The Essential Art of Communication

Lessons from the Epics and Digital Age Interactions

The Essential Art of Communication

Lessons from the Epics and Digital Age Interactions

Dr. Hema Hirlekar

Publisher
UNICORN BOOKS
F-2/16, Ansari Road, Daryaganj, New Delhi-110002
E-mail: **info@unicornbooks.in • Website: www.unicornbooks.in**
011-23275434, 23262683, 23250704

Branch : Mumbai
23-25, Zaoba Wadi, Thakurdwar, Mumbai-400002
022-22010941, 022-22053387
E-mail: **rapidex@bom5.vsnl.net.in**

ISBN: 978-81-7806-321-8
The Essential Art of Communication

Edition: 2015

Printed at : *Param Offsetters, Okhla, New Delhi-110020*

Dedicated to

Shridhar, Ashwini and Haridini

Acknowledgements

Dr. Kiran Thakur, my guide and mentor who always encouraged me.

Dr. Shriram Joshi, my friend who took the trouble of reading my manuscript and suggested a better structure to arrange the contents.

Dr. Ashok Gupta of Unicorn Books for supporting me and giving valuable suggestions. Dr. Sachchidanand Shukla of Unicorn Books for his additional inputs on Ramayana.

All my friends and well-wishers, who think I can write!

Thanks a ton!

– Dr. Hema Hirlekar

Introduction

Ramayana, the epic poem of India was originally written by Valmiki. As Indians, generally, our first glimpse into Ramayana is in the stories we have heard from our grannies. In fact, Ramayana has been told and retold in many languages all over the world and especially in Asia. These variations are rich in narrative diversity. The stories and the stories within those stories are riveting. However, those are not just stories, but they all have some precepts, some advice given cleverly.

People have culled guidelines from the epic to suit their requirements. These themes have taken Ramayana out of the time in which it was written and made it timeless. The lessons within Ramayana are as valuable today as they were when the epic poem first came into being. Apart from the ideal relationships, Ramayana has been a treasure trove for ideas about people-management, war strategies, dharma, and even women-emancipation. A historian may look for proofs; a geographer may map the movements of the main characters.

When I read Ramayana for the umpteenth time, I had a sudden 'eureka' moment! I discerned 'modern communication principles' in Ram's analysis of Hanuman's speech, uttered when Ram and Lakshman meet Hanuman for the first time. Ramayana has the most effective communicator in the legendary Hanuman. Being in the business of communication, this find spurred me on and I found more such pearls strewn all over the epic. I have managed to collect a few and string them together to share with you.

If Ramayana can advise, I was sure Mahabharata too cannot fall behind. So, from Mahabharata also, I managed to get some great key guidelines about proper speech. Maharshi Vyas, while advising Yudhishtir on the duties of a king, elaborates on proper speech by recounting a story of Tapaswini Sulabha, who spoke with king Janak of Mithila about the speech and interpersonal skills.

Surprisingly, all these epic tenets about communication are so unchanging even today, unchanging even in these times of continuous and supersonic changes in every field around us. Fast-paced technological advances, globalisation, seamless virtual world, and instant communication are the major drivers of the modern-day change. This change has affected not only the corporate environment, but also the individual one. We all have to adjust to change at both individual and work levels. Changing with the times is now a necessity to survive and prosper.

Most of us develop our own strategies to adapt to change, knowingly, unknowingly. We manage. However, at the corporate level, any change requires a deliberate approach, mainly because people instinctively oppose a change for various reasons. Forcing a change on people will create more resistance. What can facilitate a change is communication. Through proper communication, a change can be managed at personal and work level.

This book tries to address both the modern-day communication needs - interpersonal and change. The former through epic tenets and the latter through the changing rules!

—Dr. Hema Hirlekar

Contents

Part-II – Let's Talk Business!

Part-I

LET'S TALK WELL!

We all talk. Some of us more than others, but talk we do. How we talk, what we talk reveals a lot about us. Our speech can either help us achieve our goals, make our life or leave us exclaiming, *"Wish I could have asserted myself!"* We also write to communicate. Communication is the basis of human relationships, whether at home, at work or at social gatherings.

To be able to talk well, communicate effectively is, indeed, an asset. An asset that is exclusive to human beings a special gift of nature. That is what makes speech so very special. That is why amongst the five senses speech is considered the foremost. About the importance of speech, Indian scholar, Bhartrihari says in his brilliant treatise, 'Neeti-Shatak':

'Bracelets do not adorn a person. Nor do pearl necklaces shining like the moon, or a cleansing bath; nor anointment of the body, nor flowers, nor decoration for the hair. It is the cultured speech alone that embellishes a man. All other ornaments lose their glitter, only the jewel of speech ever remains the jewel of jewels.'

Cultured speech in a person is, indeed, the best ornament one can have. Nothing else matches the brilliance of correct and charming speech. Words can make a difference where strength may fail! In today's connected world, speech and writing have become vital. Expressing yourself effectively is an art! Some people are instinctively good at it, but fortunately, for the rest of us, this art can be learnt. We just have to be aware.

Interpersonal skills are the life skills we use everyday to communicate and interact with other people, both individually and in groups. Apart from effective communication, these skills include active listening and comprehension, dealing with confrontations and decision-making. Strong interpersonal skills certainly pave the way for success in professional and personal lives. People with such skills are looked upon as confident and charming.

Communication at work too is between individuals. Machines do not talk to each other! Thus, the guidelines for interpersonal and business communication do not differ much. In fact, in modern times, business communication is becoming more and more informal. The so-called 'officialese' is no longer considered proper. The phrases such as 'your good selves' and 'I remain yours truly' have now become passé. However, despite the newer tools of communication, such as e-mails, video-audio-web conferencing, IM and the social media, the fundamentals of effective communication have not changed.

Today, friends and colleagues are spread across geographies and time zones. Professionals are certainly putting all these technologies to frequent – almost constant – use. They are communicating more than ever before. It's a reflection of how people work today – and the hazy line distinguishing their business and personal lives. Regular working hours are not always adhered to, and people work beyond the regular hours more often than not, and many times, away from office too.

Interestingly, new communication tools have not replaced the old ones. There is a strong preference for utilising a mix of the traditional and new communication technologies:

- Sending IMs to get a simple question answered, scheduling an appointment
- Audio conferencing to gain consensus on an important topic

- Firing a quick text to let a colleague know they're running late

So, while newer communication tools are being utilized heavily, workers still rely on more traditional modes to be successful in their roles. Face-to-face communication still remains the preferred mode of communication for the vital tasks. For example, if the conversation is about a new project, confirming a deal or making a sensitive decision, people prefer to do it in person. Discussing complicated technical concepts and brainstorming is always better in person.

The tools of communication are evolving but the rules remain the same. The criteria of effective communication as epitomised by Hanuman in Ramayana or the guidelines of proper speech as advised by the lady ascetic, Tapaswini Sulabha in Mahabharata are still very much relevant. In fact, the fundamental 7Cs of communication are an imprint of the rules that Hanuman's speech exemplified.

Let us first have a look at what Hanuman followed in his narration and how we can utilize the lessons learnt in our daily interactions. Surprisingly, these and many other lessons relate to everyone's day-to-day life.The teachings in Ramayana encompass a vast array of subjects and issues, but we will restrict ourselves to only communication-related lessons that help in business and work communication, and hold equally true for social interactions.

Let's first know about the incidents that hold lessons for everyday communication in today's world.

Hanuman Meets Ram-Lakshman

In the epic Ramayana, Hanuman is one of the central characters, known for his strength, valour and devotion to Ram. However, that was not his whole persona. He was a scholar and a great communicator. It is told in the epic that he learnt the Vedas and other scriptures from the Sun God himself. This facet of his character comes to the fore when he meets Ram and Lakshman for the first time in the epic Ramayana.

The time is when Ravan has abducted Sita, and Ram and Lakshman are looking for her everywhere. They enter a forest near a lake called Pampa. They have royal physique and bearing, but are dressed like hermits. They are armed but do not seem threatening. The exiled monkey king, Sugreev is intrigued and also worried that his brother Vali may have sent some mercenaries to kill him. So, he asks his trusted Deputy, Hanuman to find out about these two strangers in their vicinity.

Hanuman, at the behest of Sugreev, approaches Ram and Lakshman in the guise of an ascetic Brahmin. The reason to change his original form to that of a sanyasi is to seem agreeable and so that the sight of a monkey approaching them should not put off Ram and Lakshman. Also because

Ram and Lakshman may not doubt the entry of an ascetic Brahmin in their midst.

Hanuman, thus, approaches the royal duo and begins to speak. From here up to Sundar Kanda, Hanuman's words and actions are a lesson in effective communication and need an in-depth analysis. In this episode, everything that Hanuman says is drawn from scriptures and political science, and Ram's analysis of Hanuman's speech and actions too is relevant to scriptures. In mythology, Hanuman is taken as *veda-vedaang-paarangat,* knower of all Vedas, and their subsidiary scriptures, *nava-vyaakarana-pandit,* scholar in nine schools of grammar, and *buddhimatta-varishtah,* cleverest of the clever. He is the supreme scholar, teacher, and the cleverest.

On nearing the brothers Ram and Lakshman, Hanuman approaches them respectfully and after greeting them in a soft and pleasing voice, begins to speak thus:

"You two look like royal ascetics. You could even be deities going by your bearing and physique. Your complexions are clear and fair. Your arrival in this area has scared animals and other inhabitants. However, you seem unaware of it."

"You are on the banks of Lake Pampa and you are looking at the variety of trees. Your presence has gladdened the waters of the river, due to which it flows more energetically. It shimmers with the golden hue of your radiance. You come across as highly courageous, but contrarily, you look gloomy. You look strong, yet your distress has affected all the beings in this forest."

"Dauntless, bold and brave are you with keen gaze of the lions. The bows that you carry seem akin to Lord Indra's bows, giving you an appearance of the enemy destroyers, yet your attire seems

totally at variance. You dazzle with your deportment, which is glorious, splendid, and even impetuous. You emit energy like the Sacred Bulls. Your arms resemble the elephant trunks. You radiate assurance and fortitude. The majesty of the king of mountains, that graces this forest, has multiplied with your reflected brilliance. You certainly appear worthy of being emperors or are you celestial beings? It is indeed puzzling how you have reached this countryside."

"Both of you have eyes like lotus petals, and your demeanour does not seem to be that of mere human beings. But, that surely is not possible as you sport beards and long hair tied up like ascetics. It is highly confusing, your other worldly looks and your presence here on the Earth. Is the Earth so fortunate that Sun and Moon have decided to visit her? Maybe you are powerful gods in human form! Who exactly you might be?"

"Your arms are long and your shoulders are powerful. These seem to be accustomed to royal ornaments, but, at present, sans such ornaments, you roam unaccompanied by a royal entourage, that befittingly seems to be your prerogative."

"It seems that you are the chosen ones to protect this Earth adorned with Mount Meru and Vindhya Range, and with all her oceans and forests. Your awesome bows are brilliantly polished and sparkle like Lord Indra's golden thunderbolt bow. The quivers that you carry so effortlessly on your backs are bursting with hazardous, life terminating, fiery snake like sharp arrows, admirable in their appearance. Your swords are wide, sharp and seem ready to attack like snakes that have just moulted."

"I have been speaking with you for so long, as monkey king Sugreev's emissary, and you do not respond at all!"

A monkey has limited patience. Hanuman is vexed with their silence. So far, he has been talking using all those flattering words, which he has drawn from various scriptures. Their attire and hair tufts are like those of sages and hermits; along with their self-contradictory appearance as would-have-been emperors, their mighty weaponry, and every other thing, he says, are the quotes from *'lakshanashaatra'*, the scripture that details the qualities of the great emperors. This is what has made the two listeners wonder about this ascetic!

In the midst of this unpopulated thick forest, an ascetic Brahmin approaches them, talks at length, and his speech shows familiarity with scriptures. Ram and Lakshman seem as confused about him as he seems to be about them. He is comfortably wandering in a deep forest unlike an ascetic, a role that he seems to portray. A sage would generally be found near some human habitation and not in the forests. Also an ascetic will not speak unless spoken to. However, this particular ascetic seems very keen to know the identity of the strangers in the midst of the forest. Was he a demon in disguise?

Ram does not speak but is attentive and, while listening to him, also assesses the person behind the façade. By now, Hanuman is ready to reveal himself as there is no response forthcoming.

"Delegated by the King of monkeys, the great Sugreev, I have come here. My name is Hanuman and I am also a Vanara. Sugreev is very keen to establish friendship with you two. I am his minister and emissary, Hanuman – the son of Lord Varun (God of Air). I have come from Mountain Rishyamukh in an ascetic's form on the orders of King Sugreev."

Hanuman says his piece and then speaks nothing further.

All this while, Ram listens to Hanuman and, judging by his expression, seems highly pleased. He has evaluated

Hanuman's speech and now explains his assessment to Lakshman, who stands by his side.

Following the Imperial protocol, Ram does not enter into any conversation with the emissary. Later, Ram asks Lakshman to conduct dialogue with Hanuman. Apart from the protocol, there is another reason for this. Lakshman too is a seasoned communicator and his knowledge of scriptures equals that of Hanuman. Now, Ram elaborates on his analysis of this envoy's knowledge and, consequently, his King Sugreev's qualities and explains to Lakshman in the following manner:

"Hanuman is the minister of that great King of monkeys, Sugreev. I know of him and whatever I have heard about him is worth admiring. Lakshman, oh mighty warrior, this minister of Sugreev is very eloquent and pleasant spoken and you may communicate with him."

"A person who spoke so eloquently, has to be learned in Rig Veda, has to be able to recite Yajur Veda and has to be a scholar of Saam Veda, only then can he possibly speak this way."

Hereafter, Ram's analysis of Hanuman is given.

In Rig Veda, every letter has many phonetically deflected variations, which may mean different things when used in different ways. It is practically impossible to contain that information unless the scholar has complete knowledge. Hence, Ram uses the word, *'vineet'*, which means well trained.

In Yajur Veda, many passages occur recursively, with different connotations. Remembering not to mix one with the other is a difficult process. Hence, the scholar has to have an extremely sharp memory.

In Saam Veda, the pitch and duration of the rendering is extremely important, and, as such, it requires a scholarly bent of mind to control the vocal notes.

The three aspects, 'vinaya' - schooling, 'dhaarana' - memory and 'vedana' - knowledge, are required for each of the above Vedas.

Hanuman says, *"You two are eligible to rule the earth"*, which is a quote from the Rigveda Aitereya. Next, he says, *"You are the deities in human form"*, which is a quote from Yajur Veda. Many such instances of quotations and references from the scriptures abound in Hanuman's speech.

Ram continues, *"Definitely grammar is separately and comprehensively learnt by him. He has spoken so much but not a single word is ungrammatical or amiss."*

Earlier, the Vedic knowledge of Hanuman was analysed. Now his knowledge of grammar, the essential part of Vedic learning, is analysed. Without the knowledge of subsidiary scriptures of the Vedas, such as *vyaakaran, nirukta, sikhsha, chandas,* the study of Vedas and its ancillaries itself is futile. Reading and reciting the Vedic hymns is of no use in practical life, for the knowledge garnered in such a way needs to be practically implemented in life. Hanuman implements the grammar and the training received originally as a Vedic scholar.

"On his face or eyes, on forehead or brows, or on other faculties of expression, no fault is found. Not even the least."

Now, the behavioural niceties of a Vedic scholar are being analysed. The learning of the Vedas imposes certain rules while reciting the hymns.

A verse elucidates the faults of the bad communicators:

Stretching the words unnecessarily, speaking hurriedly, nodding while speaking, just reading from the text, unaware of the meaning, weak-voiced.

Ram goes on elaborating, *"He has an orderly refinement in speech that is remarkable and undelaying, and he speaks gracious words that are pleasing. Sweet voice, properly enunciated syllables, requisite pauses between the words, quick and confident, unambiguous and rhythmic speech are the essential qualities of good communicators. Hanuman exhibits all these qualities."*

"Oh, virtuous Lakshman, if a king does not have this sort of envoy, really how can that king accomplish his objectives? With such an accomplished envoy, that king can easily get his work done with the benefit of the envoy's communication skills," Ram says to Lakshman.

❐

Hanuman and Sita's First Meeting

Another example of Hanuman's prowess as a communicator is exhibited at the time when he is assigned the task of searching for Sita. Let us briefly recount the sequence of events.

Hanuman locates Sita sitting morosely under an Ashoka tree. Her demeanour, her attire, her pathos and her tapas radiance convince him that he has found Ram's Sita. She moves under the Sinsupa tree that Hanuman is sitting upon and grasps a branch to hang herself. However, suddenly, lucky omens occur and she halts in her endeavour. Could there be a message?

Now Hanuman wonders how to approach her without frightening her. Although he is already in the form of a tiny monkey, she might take him to be an enemy, or Ravan's envoy! After much deliberation, he decides on an approach. He thinks he would praise Shri Ram and narrate a few details of the family that a rakshasa would not do. Initially, he thinks of speaking in Sanskrit, the pure language of Brahmins. Then he decides against it, as Ravan too is proficient in Sanskrit. Speaking softly in colloquial language, so as not to let the guard rakshasis overhear, he begins praising Shri Ram, gradually narrating Sita's disappearance, Ram's grief, Vali's slaying and Sugreev and Ram joining hands to search for Sita.

Sita, after initial hesitation, accepts Hanuman and seems to believe in him. Now, it is his turn to confirm that she is indeed Sita, but he cannot ask her directly lest he should sound rude. So, he says,

"One whose eyes are like lotus petals, one who has worn begrimed but silken clothes…why are you holding that branch? Why do tears keep flowing from your eyes? ...Are you some kind of Goddess? Are you Rohini? Are you Rishi Vasishtha's Arundhati? … However, by your looks and other royal signs, I feel you are Shri Ram's Sita. … If you are, tell me likewise…"

Then Sita tells him her story. Hanuman is convinced and comes nearer to Sita. In a flash, Sita repents her easy acceptance of him. She fears that this creature is Ravan in disguise or one of his sevaks! She retreats and grieves. Then, Hanuman again convinces her by giving many more details about her abduction from their ashram. He further adds that now that she is found, it was but a matter of just a few days for Ram, Lakshman and the monkeys and bears to arrive in Lanka and, after punishing Ravan, rescue Sita.

Once again, Sita is assured of Hanuman's identity as Ram's envoy. She asks him to tell her about Sugreev and his meeting with Ram and other events that followed. Hanuman does so and asks her to give some details of a past event to tell Ram, so that he knows it is really his own Sita that Hanuman found. She, in turn, recounts an incident that only she and Ram knew.

Then, Hanuman takes out the ring given to him by Ram, with the name Ram on it, to be handed over to Sita as a token. Why did he not produce the ring right at the beginning? It was the most crucial piece of evidence. But before Sita was completely certain about Hanuman's integrity, she might have taken the ring as Ravan's magic or illusion. So, finally, when she saw the ring, the lingering doubts too vanished and she was happy.

❐

Hanuman and Ravan's First Meeting

The time when Hanuman met Ravan, the king of Lanka, in his court also has lessons in communication. After destroying Ashokvan, annihilating a huge demon army and killing Ravan's five very fiery archers as well as his son Aksha, Hanuman wants to confront Ravan in person, so he lets himself be bound by Indrajeet, Ravan's son, who had defeated even Lord Indra. He is taken to the royal court in Lanka.

Ravan sees Hanuman and wonders if he was any of his past enemies in disguise? So, he asks his chief minister, Prahasta (as a king should not directly speak to an alien) to find out who he was and all his antecedents. Though Prahasta questions him, Hanuman directly addresses Ravan, denying that he was any God's emissary. He says with respect, *"I am a monkey by birth. I wanted to see you. Finding no other way, I destroyed a few trees. I killed some rakshasas in self-defence. No Astra can do me any harm. To see you, I allowed myself to be found by your people. I came as an emissary of the mighty Ram. I have some message for you, which is for your own good."*

Hanuman here takes some liberties with truth while inventing explanation for his conduct at the garden. His speech shows his tact and presence of mind. He does begin addressing Ravan in all gentleness. He neither defies

Ravan nor does he threaten him right at the start. Had he done that, what he wanted to convey about Ram would have drowned in the resulting pandemonium. He wanted complete attention of the assembly. So, he mentions self-defence while killing the rakshasas. He says that Sugreev has sent him and wished him happiness. He praises Ravan by saying, *"Sir! You know every dharma. You did great Tapasya."*

Only after he has captured complete attention of the king and the assembly, he goes on to defy Ravan and talks about Ram's greatness and valour. The diction is superb and is like a Vedic hymn in praise of Ram. Most important is that everyone listens to it without a murmur.

❐

Hanuman Meets Bharat

The war in Lanka is won, 14 years of exile are over and Ram starts back to Ayodhya with Sita, Lakshman, Hanuman and others. At Rishi Bharadwaj's ashram, Shri Ram halts and asks Hanuman to go ahead to Ayodhya to narrate all that had happened to Bharat and ask about his welfare, and, while doing so, to observe his facial expressions and judge carefully if he has even a slight desire to continue to rule the country. In that case, Hanuman was to come back and tell Ram, so that Ram would go back and not claim the kingdom.

At a distance of two miles from Ayodhya, Hanuman sees Bharat, living in a hermitage, with the bark trees and dressed in a deerskin, emaciated, wearing matted locks on his head, his limbs coated with dirt. Hanuman sees his suffering and knows that it is due to the separation from Ram, his elder brother. So, now instead of narrating the happenings and asking him about his well-being, Hanuman immediately tells Bharat of Ram's return. This suddenly makes Bharat swoon in happiness and then, gradually, Hanuman goes on to recount the happenings. He knows Bharat has absolutely no desire for the kingdom, so he doesn't return to Ram.

Hanuman knew that right at that moment Bharat would not be in a frame of mind to listen to the lengthy narratives about the happenings. All that he would be interested in knowing was if and when was his beloved Ram to return. In fact, as 14 years of Ram's exile are over and there is no news from Ram, Bharat is planning to enter into the fire to end his life. It is really imperative that Bharat learns about Ram's eminent arrival. So, Hanuman tells him about that and then the rest of the saga.

In fact, while narrating the happenings, Hanuman very prudently omits the mention of Sita's fire ordeal. He did not want to offend the sensibilities of the already suffering Bharat. Or, maybe, he did not wish Bharat to misinterpret Ram's action.

❒

Hanuman Disagrees with the Monkey Leaders in the Case of Vibhishan

Again, in another situation in Ramayan, Hanuman displays his excellent reasoning and power of analysis. Vibhishan, with four of his trusted aides, leaves Ravan and comes to Ram. Feeling the hostility of the monkey chiefs around Ram, he conveys loudly that he has left the wicked Ravan, his elder brother and has come to Ram for protection. He wishes to assist Ram in his war against Ravan.

Will his surrender be accepted? Ram has an emergency discussion with his generals. All advise against taking Vibhishan, suggesting to first observe his conduct, giving him a task to judge his sincerity, to send a spy to question his intentions, to know why such wrong place and time for surrender was chosen by him. All this time, Hanuman is silent. When Ram asks him, he responds giving his analytical reasoning, point by point. After saying that, he wished neither to excel the previous speakers nor advise Ram.

"But, we cannot observe the conduct of the rakshas as there is no time. We cannot entrust him any task for the same reason. We cannot send a spy to an enemy who is right in front of us. We cannot question him because if he has come as a friend, he will get

offended, and if he is not a friend, then questioning him will not reveal much. His timing and place too is right as even after telling Ravan to abide by Dharma, he insulted Vibhishan. So, Vibhishan must have thought it safe to distance himself from Ravan when the battle is near. Further, he must have heard that you crowned Sugreev as the king after killing Vali. He definitely wants to be the king of Lanka through you. So, he rightly came here. Again, I find nothing suspicious about him. His face is calm and amiable. His speech also is quite innocent. He is reliable and good and worthy of acceptance. A villain will never approach us so boldly and so freely. I have no suspicion about him."

For the fear that his advice may appear biased, Hanuman does not mention Vibhishan coming to his help in Ravan's court. He goes on to say, *"I think he can be safely admitted into our company. But Ram! It is all left to you."*

❐

Tapaswini Sulabha's Suggestions for Proper Speech

In the 'Shantiparva' of the epic Mahabharat, a wise and senior person, Bhishma is advising Yudhishthir after his ascension to the throne. While responding to a question by the eldest Pandav, the elder cites an example of a king named Dharmadhwaj in the Janak dynasty in Mithila. He refers to a conversation between King Janak and a tapaswini named Sulabha. After listening to the King castigating her, she decides to enlighten him about proper speech.

Sulabha says, *"O king, speech ought always to be free from the nine verbal faults and the nine faults of judgement. It should also, while setting forth the meaning with lucidity, be possessed of the eighteen well-known merits."*

"Five characteristics relating to the sense constitute the credibility of what is said. These are ambiguity, ascertainment of the faults and the merits of premises and conclusions, weighing the relative strength or weakness of those faults and merits, establishment of the conclusion, and the element of persuasiveness or otherwise that attaches to the conclusion thus arrived at."

She then expounds on these five characteristics at length.

"Saukshmyam *literally means minuteness. A word or a sentence can have many overt and covert meanings. The intellect has to comprehend the right meaning as per the context. This quality of ease or difficulty of understanding is very important. When there is confusion and only a process of elimination can lead to the correct meaning, then the fault is of minuteness or ambiguity."*

"Sankhya *is the establishment of meaning by elimination of faults or merits in assumptions and conclusions."*

"Krama *means fixing the order of the words in a sentence, depending on the relative strength or weakness of the faults or merits (ascertained by the above process)."*

"Vinirnay *means after proper analysis when, at the end of the sentence, it can be said with certainty that this is as is."*

"Desire or dislike can give rise to sorrow. Ungratified desire or just hatred can become a source of pain. To remove this pain, a person adopts some measures. This method of taking measures is known as Prayojanam."

Sulabha then proceeds, *"Be assured, O king, that when these five characteristics occur together, they constitute a complete and intelligible sentence. By occurrence of these five characteristics together is meant that only when a speaker or writer properly attends to these, only then can his sentence be said to be complete and intelligible."*

"The words should be fraught with sense, free from ambiguity (in consequence of each of them not being symbols of many things), logical, free from pleonasm (the use of more words than are necessary to express an idea) redundancy, (for example, free gift or true fact) or tautology (needless repetition of an idea, especially in words other than those of the immediate context, without imparting additional force or clarity), smooth, certain, free from bombast, agreeable or sweet, truthful, not inconsistent with the aggregate of three (viz., Righteousness, Wealth and Pleasure), refined (i.e., free

from Prakriti), not elliptical or imperfect, destitute of harshness or difficulty of comprehension, characterised by due order, not far-fetched in respect of sense, corrected with one another as cause and effect and each having a specific object."

"Speech should not be prompted by desire or wrath or fear or cupidity or abjectness or deceit or shame or compassion or pride."

"When the speaker, the hearer, and the words said, thoroughly agree with one another in the course of a speech, then does the sense or meaning come out very clearly. When, in the matter of what is to be said, the speaker shows disregard for the understanding of the hearer by uttering words whose meaning is understood only by himself, then, however good those words may be, they become incapable of being seized by the hearer. Parartham *means of excellent sense. That speaker, again, who, uncaring for his own meaning, uses words that sound good, awakens only erroneous impressions to the hearer. Such words in such connection become certainly faulty. That speaker, however, who employs words that are, while expressing his own meaning, intelligible to the hearer as well, truly deserves to be called a speaker."*

❐

Epic Lessons in Today's World

It is quite surprising how a small incident in the epic Ramayana can teach us so much about communication. Even more enlightening is Ram's analysis of Hanuman's communication skills. Now, let us take a detailed and close look at this analysis. Interestingly, the well-acclaimed 'Seven Cs of Communication' find an echo in Hanuman's communication skills. Or, maybe, Hanuman's skills are reflected in the Seven Cs of Communication. These are:

1. Completeness
2. Correctness
3. Conciseness
4. Consideration
5. Concreteness
6. Clarity
7. Courteousness

Whether writing or speaking, these 7 Cs will certainly make your communication much more effective. During the daily social interactions, it may not be possible to think, remember and implement these C-guidelines. However, except for 'completeness' and 'concreteness', all the other pointers should be easy to apply.

When you are making a speech at formal occasions or in official meetings, these guidelines will ensure that your words have a great impact. Written communication will certainly benefit by keeping in mind these guidelines.

Let us have a detailed look at the 7Cs.

Completeness

Hanuman had extensive knowledge of the Vedas - scriptures - and that essentially made his message complete, as he knew exactly what to say. His speech contained all the necessary information pertaining to the occasion and his need. His king wished to know exactly what was the intention of these two persons, whose very appearance screamed contrariness. Hanuman's speech, as we have seen, was complete, in that he elaborated on the seeming anomalies in their appearance and asked the purpose behind their presence in the Sundarban forest.

When you initiate a conversation, communication is effective or complete when it contains all the necessary information the audience needs for the result you desire. While this may sound simple, it can be challenging to try to interpret the audience's viewpoints before you craft the message. How can you be sure? Put yourself in the audience's position. Can you think of any more information that you would like to have? Or some more material that might be of use?

When you need to request information or place an order, the well-known method of answering the relevant five Ws comes in handy - why, what, when, where and to whom. In addition, of course, 'how' also features in this list! Ask for all the information you wish while giving details that might be necessary to fulfil or aid to the query.

For example, you want to make a reservation for a table in a restaurant. You need not answer 'why'! However, while talking to the reservation person, you say that you would be visiting their restaurant for the first time because you heard their food/service is really great. Or, if not, the first time you just mention that you love the food, so you keep visiting the place. This information may not be required but it creates a nice feeling and the receiver of the communiqué will remember you.

You will, of course, need to impart the necessary information: 'a table for six, away from the kitchen door, in the non-smoking area, at 8.30 PM for Seema Subramanian'.

In another instance, you wish to initiate an enquiry for a solar water heater. You cannot just say, "I want a solar heater."If you do not give all the required information in the very first instance, there will be many back and forth missives and there will be unnecessary delays. So, what should your enquiry contain?

- Is it for residential or commercial use?
- How big should the solar panels be? That will depend on your estimated usage and your water tank. So, provide the relevant details.
- Will the water heated by the solar heater be used exclusively for bathrooms?
- Will this water be used in the kitchen?
- Will the washing machine be attached to it?
- What are the options available?
- What is the price range?
- When should the delivery take place?

- Where should it be delivered?
- To whom should it be addressed?
- In addition to this, do not forget to provide your contact details and convenient time to call.
- This kind of big purchase needs face-to-face communication too. At that time, your queries should include - Who will fix the panels? Where can it be fixed? Will the installation charges be separate or included in the quote? How can the payment be made - cheque, cash, or credit card? What kinds of warranties are given? Is there any government scheme for payment, considering this is environment-friendly?

How to be Complete?

When you are responding to a mail/letter/enquiry, the authors, Murphy and Hildebrandt say that:

1. Provide all the necessary information
2. Answer all the questions asked
3. Give something extra when desirable

For example, let us say that you take orders for birthday cakes. There is a telephonic enquiry by a new customer to place an order for a birthday cake. You could just take the order and execute it. However, if you provide any additional services, now is the time to talk about it.

"Thank you for your order. You will certainly be happy with the Spiderman cake for a three-year-old that you have ordered. I also make chocolates and novel desserts that kids love. The chocolates could be used to add to the return gift-bags. The desserts are yummy and come in flavours children love like chocolate, strawberry, vanilla... would you like to order any of these? I am

sure you will love the goodies. I get many repeat orders for these chocolates and desserts."

So, your enquiries and responses both need to be complete. Especially, in written communication, research has proved that the receiver forms an opinion about the writer based on the communiqué. This should be favourable and will be if the message is complete and should come across as credible.

Credibility is a perceived quality, one that people assign to you based on the interplay of a number of elements. Your communication, written or oral, will come across as credible if you can show that you care about the other person and have their best interests at heart. You can also show that you are similar to them by using their language, body language, dress, etc. To be credible, you need to be assertive without being intimidating. Another way to be credible is to highlight the credibility of your sources of information. Credibility is tied to information, and can, thus, be described as a communication phenomenon.

Since credibility cannot be actually measured, perceived credibility will help form an opinion about the sender of the missive in the mind of the receiver. There are three qualities that may result in a person being perceived as more caring: understanding, empathy, and responsiveness.

Understanding means knowing another person's ideas, feelings and needs. Some people seem to get to the point when we communicate with them. They seem to know what we are talking about, what we are thinking. Others seem to be less sensitive. They do not recognise when our feelings are hurt or when we have a problem. We certainly feel closer to the former type of individuals.

Empathy is one person's identification with another person's feelings, when one person accepts another's feelings as valid, even if they may not approve of them.

Responsiveness is one person acknowledging another person's communicative attempts, how quickly he or she reacts, how attentive one is to the other and the degree with which one appears to listen to the other person.

Complete information in your communication builds credibility.

Correctness

Hanuman was learned in grammar and as Ram pointed out, there was not a single mistake in his speech, either of grammar or of fact.

Make sure your message is correct, and double-check that you are using proper grammar, spelling and punctuation in written communication. Even in today's SMS language, a grammatically correct writing technique stands out. Likewise, it is equally important to use accuracy in pronunciation when delivering your message verbally. Apart from grammar, even the facts and figures have to be accurate.

Correctness Counts

There is no substitute to correct grammar, spelling and punctuation. Some people may not give too much importance to grammatical errors but they may misinterpret your message like, for example, the placing of one comma can completely change the meaning of a sentence. For instance, 'Panda who eats, shoots and leaves!' It is not a gun-trotting, trigger-happy panda. The sentence should read 'Panda who eats shoots and leaves'.

When the readers encounter what they think of as mistakes, they find it hard to read your writing. They may become confused, and, if not, they may take time to actually fathom what your error-ridden message means. This time spent will take away their enjoyment in reading your message or delay their response.

People familiar with grammar, spelling and punctuation might subconsciously discard your message (even though it is acceptable and important) only because they may think that just because you are careless with grammar, you might very well be careless in other areas too. This feeling may make them question your judgement. This is not fair but it is common. There's a perception in our society, however inaccurate it may be, that people, who do not write correctly, are not very smart, and that people, who are not very smart, are not worth listening to. Both of these prejudices are wrong, but they exist nonetheless, and we should be aware of them.

How to be correct?

- The first important rule is to use the right level of language in speech and in writing. In today's fast-paced world, language suffers a lot. It is always a good idea to ensure that your language is not only of the right level, but also correct grammatically too. Also, you should remember that the 'spell check' on your computer is not a 'language check'.

Level of language

Formal, informal and conversational are the three levels of language. Sub-standard also may be added as one more type! Today, yet another language is emerging – SMS language.

In our personal or professional lives, we do not use formal language. It is mostly reserved for doctoral writings, government high-level papers, legal documents, scholarly articles, research papers and so on. It uses scholarly vocabulary, longer, more complex sentences, use of one instead of you, and a highly serious tone. There are no colloquialisms and scrupulously correct grammar. First person references are absent. There are no contractions, passive voice, no jargon, no queries, no abbreviations, and no exclamation points.

For example, instead of 'we are concerned that', it would be 'there has been concern that'.

Formal level of language is not recommended for official correspondence/e-mails. It will also take time to write and to decipher. The receiver might just decide that it is too much of an effort to figure out the content.

Informal style is the appropriate style for regular correspondence, e-mails, speech, presentations, letters and conversation. It can have contractions, can use the first and second person pronouns, I and you, simpler vocabulary, and shorter sentences. Informal, however, does not mean 'casual'!

In business writing, it is best to go straight to the point: here are the facts and this is what we need to do. Having said that, there is no need to be boring and uninteresting! It should be attractive, appealing and should hold the recipient's interest.

Business writing has only two goals:

1. To make people understand what exactly you want.
2. To urge them to take some action.

In written communication, body language plays no part. Hence, your writing has to be absolutely precise and complete. The reader consciously or subconsciously forms an opinion about the sender of the message. You should avoid officious, complex language and stick to simple but complete statements. Many people make the mistake of equating good writing with convoluted writing peppered with fantastic phrases. Such writing could annoy the reader while trying to make sense of the bombastic language or worse, make him confused and misinterpret the writing. Use simple language; vary the length of your sentences. Preferably, don't make all your sentences of the same length.

To be correct:

- State your purpose;
- List the main points;
- Use short sentences and paragraphs;
- Avoid jargon.

In writing, plain is beautiful. The next time you want someone to understand your writing, put away the fancy words and convoluted sentences. Say it simply. It will save your time, the reader's time, and your company's money.

Most people use colourful (not complicated) language when they speak: they tell stories with details, colours and smells. Write the same way. Use words to evoke images in your readers' mind, not to force them to decipher intangible concepts. If you have numbers, use them. Don't discuss ideas without examples. Avoid abbreviations that are not generally known. Everybody understands words that apply to everyday life, so use everyday words and your reader will understand you.

Factually correct:

Good writing is correct in technique as well as facts. Your facts must be absolutely correct. Verify again before committing them in writing.

If you have relevant information, present it. If you are not sure about something, admit it. If you merely suspect something, make the suspicion clear, so your reader does not think you know more than you do. Check your letter properly, at least once, before you send it. This will save a lot of trouble and awkwardness later on.

Conciseness

Hanuman's speech was 'un-delaying'. He did not speak anything in excess of the need. His words were quick and to the point. His message was not verbose, but he stated all that he had to say.

'Conciseness' means saying what needs to be said in the minimum number of words. These days people suffer from time poverty. They try to address as many communication needs and demands as possible in the time available to them. They do not have time to sort through a lot of clutter. This situation is going to get worse and worse. So, you need to remember two things. First is to make your message concise. Second, it is even more crucial to make it easy for the listener/viewer to respond. Only then will fully involved communication occur.

Effective communication succeeds without being too wordy. Say or write as little as possible to get your point across, and your message will be easier to comprehend.

In a social encounter, you tend to stay clear of the long-winded raconteur. So, why emulate such a person in writing? Like the party bore, long sentences and paragraphs cannot sustain the reader's interest for a long time. You do not want the reader to stop reading even before you have made your point! In run-on sentences and paragraphs, the reader struggles to keep from getting lost. Clear writing doesn't divert from the main point. It, in fact, offers shortcuts to understanding.

At every stage of writing your letter, read what you have written and decide what to delete without harming the meaning. Remember that you want your reader to understand you and take action. Anything that does not help in this process is unnecessary. Avoid repeating anything, other than for specific emphasis. Remove needless words from every sentence, needless sentences from every paragraph, and needless paragraphs entirely. A concise message saves the sender's and the receiver's time. However, remember that brevity at the cost of entirety is not advisable. Concise does not mean incomplete.

How to be concise?

1. Avoid wordy expressions and repetitions
2. Absolutely avoid business-speak
3. Use brief, to-the-point sentences to include only relevant material
4. Start by writing your main point, and then describe it in short
5. Cut the jargon and avoid buzzwords
6. Read aloud, mistakes generally pop up

Avoid wordy expressions and repetitions

- Use single words instead of long phrases
- Do away with unnecessary expressions and over-the-top politeness

- Substitute simple sentences for verbose statements
- Avoid passive voice unless absolutely necessary
- Do away with 'which' and 'that' clauses
- Use long names once and then use short names, abbreviations or pronouns
- Cut out repetitions
- Absolutely avoid business-speak
- Use precise, everyday substitutes for business words, for example, use 'find out' instead of 'ascertain', 'plan' instead of 'strategize'!

Use brief, to-the-point sentences to include only relevant material

- Stay within the purpose of the letter/speech
- Include only relevant information and do not repeat what the reader/audience already knows
- Do away with long-winded introductions, superfluous explanations, superfluous adjectives
- Start by writing your main point, and then describe it in short
- Get to the main purpose of the communiqué quickly
- Describe it concisely and tactfully
- Do not sacrifice completeness and clarity for conciseness
- Keep in mind the flow and tone

Cut the jargon and avoid buzzwords

- Use jargon only when the audience is from the same professional field, but not for generalised audience

- Buzzwords should be avoided completely

Read aloud, mistakes generally pop-up

- A simple method of knowing if you have used unnecessary words and repetitions
- Trust your ear. Wherever your writing is stuffy, wordy, or impersonal, rewrite it
- Ask yourself if you would say to your reader what you are writing

Consideration

Recognising the strangers in the forest for what they might be, Hanuman crafts his message with their status in mind. He considers the presentation of his point and utilises the style that would be appropriate. Realising that the strangers seem to be of royal blood and learned, he quotes from the Vedas and scriptures to substantiate his point. He is respectful but not subservient.

How to be considerate?

- Look at the things from the reader's point
- Show the reader the benefit and emphasise what s/he wants to know
- Protect the reader's ego
- Focus on the positive
- Humanise your messages
- Use proper etiquette in all communication media
- Avoid 'you' when criticising

Look at the things from the receiver's point of view

Always craft your message with the receiver in mind. It shows that you understand your audience, which goes a long way in getting your desired result. Consideration simply means you show empathy in your communication style. It also means that the message needs to be crafted with the receiver's profile in mind. For example, if you are an engineer, avoid too technical words when communicating with HR or with a client, who may be non-technical. He may not understand too much technical jargon. In fact, non-comprehension may put him off. Here the message needs to be simple and direct, with the purpose of communication made clear.

Remember not to lose your temper, and avoid accusatory tone.

Show the reader benefit

The important point to remember is to focus on 'you' and not on 'I' or 'we'. Most of the messages can be turned around to make them audience-oriented. Sometimes, the real benefit may be for you, but it is easy to turn any phrase around and make it sound like the most important person in the correspondence is, undoubtedly, the reader.

In most business situations, the reader and the writer have something to gain or lose. Focusing on the readers' benefit will make the recipients feel that you have their best interests at heart. You empathise with their point of view. It is more than just using the pronoun 'you'. A change in your attitude to really think of the reader as the most important person will go a long way in convincing them of your good intentions. Such a reader-centric attitude will actually come forth in your communication. The goal of communication is to get the audience to do what we want them to do, so we have to ensure that they believe they are valued and appreciated.

A sentence such as *"We are pleased to offer you a 10% discount on cash purchases"* has a patronising tone, and the readers are unmoved. Rouse their interest by rewriting the sentence: *"You can get a 10% discount on cash purchases."* Here is another example. The 'We-approach': *"We wish to inform you that we have despatched the book you ordered."* You-approach: *"You will receive your book tomorrow."*

The first question that pops into a reader's mind, generally, is, *"What's in it for me?"* The writers should, therefore, point to the benefit that the reader gets from acting upon the message. Benefits must meet the recipients' needs, address their concerns, or offer them rewards. Even when there is no visible benefit, the message can show interest in and concern for the reader's needs. Instead of *"We are pleased to inform you that we have opened a branch on M.G. Road and provided parking"*, you may write: *"Now enjoy the wonderful experience of shopping at our newly opened branch at M.G. Road without the hassles of finding a parking space!"*

In some cases, this can be accomplished by emphasis; you may downplay your own feelings to make a point. The readers tend to react positively when the benefits are shown to accrue to them.

Protect the receiver's ego

Most people understand far more words than they use, either in writing or speech. However, it is a good plan to maintain the same level of language throughout the writing or speech. The 'you-attitude' recognises that communication takes place between real persons, not between robots. The language, therefore, should be personal, simple and direct. Do not talk down and use heavy words such as 'obfuscate','imbroglio' and 'conflation' even if you know the meanings. Nobody likes to refer to a dictionary in daily interactions.

Even when you write/speak to tell the audience something that they do not know, there is no need to sound clever. Just remember that the audience may be uninformed about that particular point but not dumb. Also keep in mind that they may know something else you might not be even aware of!

Avoid calling your readers stupid (even if done unintentionally)

When a customer complains about some equipment that you supplied is not working, there is no need to say, *"If you had read the instruction booklet..."* or *"You are probably ignorant of the fact that..."* Just enquire whether they have gone through the booklet and show how to rectify the problem.

Avoid suggesting that they are lying (even if you don't say so directly)

You may think the customer is lying; still avoid saying, *"You claim that you returned the item."* Or with a smirk, *"According to you, the computer stopped working!"*

Avoid indicating that they are complainers

Not too many people take kindly to being labelled 'complainers' even if they are! Instead of *"You complain that..."*, you could say, *"I understand that..."*.

Instead of *"We have received your complaint regarding the service at our hotel..."*, you could modify the sentence to, *"We are grateful that you have pointed out the lacunae in our service..."*

Focus on the positive

Positive emphasis focuses on what can be done and not on what can't be done. When you emphasise the positive, you convince the reader that you are goal-oriented. When you emphasise the negative, you sound unsure and indecisive.

How to ensure positive emphasis?

Is there a 'not' in your message? Change immediately and replace it with a positive phrase. The meaning remains the same but the negative tone changes into positive. Try using 'only if' instead of 'not unless' and 'decline' instead of 'not accept'.

These are some words that can immediately spark a negative response in the audience. Avoid such words that either deny such as – no, do not, refuse, and stop, or convey unhappy or unpleasant associations such as – unfortunately, unable to, cannot, mistake, problem, error, damage, loss, failure, afraid, regret, argue, should, blame, complain, delay, fail, fault, it is not my responsibility... in fact, if you just go through your message once, you will be able to pick out such words, if any.

On the other hand, there are some words that immediately place the audience in a positive frame of mind – for example, agree, increase, positive, best opportunity, confident, new, achieve, fresh, improve, good....

Express your ideas in positive terms

The audience have to figure out the action that they are supposed to take and, if stated positively, the expected response can be immediate. This means stressing what can be done instead of what cannot be done. If you tell them what they can't do, they have to figure out what they can do. Make it easy for them; say what they can do!

Avoid: Don't forget to submit your expenses.

Say: Please remember to submit your expenses.

The use of 'you' in negative situations can be avoided by employing passive voice, making the receiver a part of the group.

Another way to show consideration is to emphasize on the pleasant and positive facts. Also, you must focus on the words your recipient considers favourable.

Humanise your audience

Whenever we begin to write some official letter or make some speech/presentation, most of us tend to forget the conversational language and slip into the official language. However, the receiver is a human being. So, why use some high flaunting terms?

We all need to feel that people notice and appreciate our good efforts.

In a broad but true sense, consideration underlies the other six Cs of good business communication. You adapt your language and message content to your receiver's needs when you make your message complete, concise, concrete, clear, courteous and correct.

Concreteness

Hanuman's message did not get lost in generalities. He was specific and his use of words was pleasing. He did quote from the scriptures but only to validate his point, not to show off his knowledge. He used just the right amount of details and painted vivid pictures with his speech. Just have a look!

"You two look like royal ascetics. You could even be deities going by your bearing and physique. Your complexions are clear and fair. Your arrival in this area has scared the animals and other inhabitants. However, you seem unaware of it."

"... Your presence has gladdened the waters of the river due to which it flows more energetically. It shimmers with the golden hue of your radiance. You come across as highly courageous, but, contrarily, you look gloomy. You look strong yet your distress has affected all the beings in this forest."

"...The bows that you carry seem akin to Lord Indra's bows giving you an appearance of the enemy destroyers, yet your attire seems totally at variance.You dazzle with your deportment, which is glorious, splendid, and even impetuous. ... You radiate assurance and fortitude. ... You certainly appear worthy of being emperors or are you celestial beings? It is indeed puzzling how you have reached this countryside!"

"...It is highly confusing, your other-worldly looks and your presence here on the Earth. Is the Earth so fortunate that Sun and Moon have decided to visit her? Maybe you are powerful Gods in human form! Who exactly you might be?"

How Lord Hanuman brings his words alive! The descriptions are taken from the scriptures but used in the right context. The words help to show a glimpse of his knowledge without any arrogance or excessive details. Also his speech justifies the reason for his bewilderment at their presence in the forest. Yet, there are no unnecessary minutiae that confuse.

Concrete vs. Abstract

We lead our lives in the concrete, not abstract. Our day is made up of definite facts and not just abstract ideas. It's easier for us to understand the concrete and, as a consequence, remember it.

Concrete details are a common ground at a shared level of understanding. When you drive a car, you probably do not know the automobile mechanism. You do know how to change gears, use the brake/accelerator – these are physical realities, but you may not know how the motor functions (unless, of course, it is your subject or passion!) as this needs abstract knowledge of the subject.

This common ground is one reason that metaphor, simile, and analogy work so well. They associate your idea with concrete details of something you already know.

Hey, but didn't we say that knowledge is essential? Yes, we did! The abstract concepts are required when you study the subject. However, your listeners may not be experts and have no wish to be! So, they need to know your abstract concept in concrete everyday terms, in a language they will understand.

In written and spoken communication, knowledge is essential; it is true! Without certain knowledge, how can you make your point understood? But remember that you understand the subject and the pattern, while your audience may not be so conversant with the subject. In fact, because you know the subject well, you have the ability to put it in simple words, in plain language.

For example, my engineer husband gives directions, *"...when you come to the first motorable road, take a 45-degree turn due east..."* For a layperson like me (who is also directionally challenged!), all this is Latin and Greek! For me, motorable road is any cross-country like a muddy track, whereas he meant tar-road! 45-degree turn due east? How about half right turn?

You need to communicate in a language your audience understands if you want them to understand your message. That understood language is the language of the concrete detail. It's a shared context. It has the same frame of reference for all of us.

Concrete is vivid!

Vivid imagery, colourful descriptions, yet simple words... it is tricky but not difficult. How to achieve this? When you write, imagine writing to a specific person, when you give a speech, imagine a specific listener. Also carry your imagination further and think of your audience as someone who does not have the detailed knowledge you have. There are exceptions of course, for instance, when you are talking to people from your field!

Making things concrete makes them real. Expressing your ideas vividly makes your audience actually see, hold your idea and feel it. Concrete is also specific people doing specific things. Make connections between your ideas and real people. Use examples and case studies. Create identities for your audience instead of thinking of them as an abstract group of people.

The more specific details you use, the more credible the story becomes. You don't necessarily need to go overboard and pepper too many details. Concreteness relies more on providing the *right* detail for the intended audience. Concrete details allow us to imagine a scene and, crucially, imagine ourselves in it. This immediately creates empathy.

Add colour...

Language experts say that one of the strongest ways to create visual impact is to use colour in your descriptions. This almost forces your reader/listener to paint a mental picture, which anchors your idea in his consciousness.

Associating an idea with a colour is a great way to tie up a particular thought or fact in your audience's memory. The impression you make will be more vivid and more enduring. Just think red tomatoes, green lawn, and orange sunset!

Add action...

As we have seen, ideas are not some abstract concepts. They need to be effective. Think about what exactly you want your reader/listener to do when you are expressing an idea. Do you wish to prompt some action? Inspire some thought? Accept an offer? Then put that action into words, let them visualise the idea and let your words motivate them to take the desired action.

How to be concrete?

- Be specific
- Active and not passive
- Use facts and figures whenever desirable
- Use vivid, colourful words
- Put action in your words

Be specific

Communication should be explicit and specific. In any language, there are many connotative words. Best is to avoid using them unless absolutely imperative. Denotative words are specific and they create no confusion in the audience's mind.

Active and not passive

Using active voice makes your sentences action-oriented. People act and interact. The active voice is vigorous, brief, produces more forceful tone, shows who acts and how. In passive sentences, things are done; people are acted upon or, worse, conveniently disappear. In most contexts, the passive voice is vague and evasive, making your reader unsure who is doing what.

Using the active voice usually produces a sense that the message is direct (to-the-point), people are an important part of the 'equation', the action is more dynamic, there is more immediacy (happening now), and, in general, that the message is more sincere and forceful.

For business communication, the active voice is usually the better choice, and should dominate. After all, business communication is mostly about people doing things with each other, building trust, and being efficient.

Many of us still write much too formally for general communication purposes; consequently, we shift automatically to the passive voice. We need to consciously steer away from that tendency. We need to adapt to the modern tone of business writing, which is a lot more personal and informal than it was 30 years ago. So, get personal, get straight! Build credibility. Don't let the words dominate your ideas. Be active. Look at the reader directly. Let the reader perceive your sincerity.

However, sometimes, passive voice has its uses:

It is most effective for minimizing the role of the person performing an action, or for leaving out the actor altogether, when the action, and not the individual, is the crucial point. That is why people like to use the passive voice when writing reports; they can completely avoid identifying who is responsible for a situation!

"The failure in the bridge supports was due to the fact that the bridge had not been regularly inspected."

When you want to avoid personal blunt accusations:

"The October check was not included" is more tactful than "You failed to include...."

"Attendance at the meeting is required" is less hard than "You must attend...."

The passive voice is a great way to hide critical information:

"This decision was taken yesterday."

The message can be even more abbreviated and obtuse:

"This decision was taken." (But by whom, when, and....)

Even if we include the missing information, the emphasis is deflected from the issue of who took the decision.

"This decision was taken yesterday by one of my senior managers."

Use facts and figures whenever possible

Facts in any message are difficult to deny. However, you have to be absolutely sure of the statistics you quote.

Also using facts allows you to have a strong starting point. As an example, let us say that you have an architectural firm. You already have a successful project of designing a school building. Refer to that project; quote real reviews and positive comments in your brochure or when you are addressing potential clients. (If the reviews are not positive, do not mention anything about them. Just emphasise upon the experience.)

Writing articles with a number of facts in them establishes your own credibility and the credibility of your product or service. What needs did you see that prompted you to create the product? Each fact-focused statement communicates differently, and each serves to explain the benefits of your product or service.

Include relevant statistics that support your argument. Remember to always have more facts and figures than you think you will need. And ensure that your data is up to the minute. By using concrete facts and figures, you can ensure that your receivers know exactly what is desired. When you supply specifics for the reader, you increase the likelihood that your message will be interpreted the way you intended.

Being concrete also means you provide most of the value (from the perspective of the reader/listener/viewer, not necessarily from your perspective) in the least amount of time and space. This will hold their complete attention, which again is a limited resource in this fast-paced world!

Use vivid, image-building words and put action in your verbs

Verbs

- 'He walked into the room.' is fine, but it does not create an image. Similar verbs but with more impact and visual appeal are tiptoed, stomped, sauntered, crept, rushed, waltzed.
- 'The girls talked.' How about chatted noisily, whispered, conversed, shouted?
- 'The man drove away in his car' or 'The man sped away in his Sedan'.

Verbs describe the action in a sentence. That is the intended purpose of 'verbs'. So, it is better that the actions are in verbs, not in nouns! Some verbs are stronger than other words with similar meaning, and these will make your writing more effective. For example, 'I got scared!' and 'I got petrified!' Don't you think 'scared' is milder than 'petrified'? 'Petrified' indicates that I was so scared that I was almost paralysed! The adverb (or the adverbial phrase) is a bonus; the action and a description of the action are packed into one tiny word. That's what makes it stronger: it's a single word that contains the meaning of an entire group of words!

You need details that are vivid and compelling. And they have to matter to your reader. Learn the art of using concrete detail and you'll learn how to get your audience keen to do what you intend them to do.

The 'be' word in writing can take the action away from the verb. Whenever possible, change the 'be' verb into action verb. Once you get the hang of it, this becomes a habit. For instance, instead of 'she was on the road', how about 'she walked/stood on the road'? Avoiding the 'be' verb as much as possible will add action to your verbs.

You can make your message forceful by using:

Comparisons - 'She has become smarter' is less impressive than 'She has become twice as smart as she was earlier!'

Sensory appeals - Writing comes alive if you appeal to the readers' five senses. Like a ferocious dog, scowling villain, very tall and thin (visual), the chiming bells (auditory).

Figurative language - Figurative language means using a word or phrase that departs from everyday literal language for the sake of comparison, emphasis, clarity or freshness. Metaphor and simile are the two most commonly used figures of speech, but things like hyperbole, synecdoche, puns, and personification are also figures of speech.

When used with caution and precision, these writing devices can be a powerful tool to get your point across vividly, clearly and with elegance, while adding flair and pizzazz to your writing.

Similes and metaphors compare two objects or ideas to enhance description. They help us understand the unknown by comparing or contrasting it to ideas we are more familiar with.

Similes say an object or idea is like another one, by using words such as 'like' or 'as'. Similes are often used to say that one thing is like something else, looks like something else, or does the same thing as something else, like, *"It's hot as an oven in here."* or *"Her smile was like sunshine."*

Metaphors are more direct. They say one thing is another. Metaphors make the reader use more of their imagination to the make the full connection the writer is expressing. For example, we can turn the above similes into metaphors: *"This room is an oven."* or *"Her smile is sunshine."*

Personification is when we bring ideas and objects to life by treating them as though they were human. For example, "Unseen, in the background, Fate was quietly slipping the lead into the boxing gloves." (P.G. Wodehouse, *Very Good, Jeeves,* 1930). *"Opportunity knocked on the door!"*

Synecdoche refers to using a part or piece of something to refer to the whole. This device is used widely in regular conversations so it can give a lot of warmth to your writing. 'I am all ears!' 'That's a nice set of wheels!'

A hyperbole is an exaggeration that is so dramatic that no one would believe the statement is true. 'He was so hungry; he ate everything, plate and all.'

Onomatopoeia is to use a word to describe or imitate a natural sound or the sound made by an object or an action. Example: snap, crackle, pop.

Clarity

Hanuman's message was clear and unambiguous. Despite their regal bearing, they were dressed like hermits, so what were they doing in the forest? He used the right level of language and there was no chance of misinterpreting his words.

Communicating with clarity means getting the message through to your audience clearly so that they do not misinterpret the meaning or misconstrue what you are trying to say. Be sure to use the right level of language for your audience, whether communicating verbally or through the written word.

Clarity is not merely a matter of efficiency, or of saying a lot with few words, but of accurately describing what matters in a way simple and compelling enough for others to act on. Clarity in business is essential, as the environment is ambiguous enough as it is. This is readily reflected in the use of jargon and corporate double speak. Clarity is an excellent strategy for dealing with corporate complexity.

Basic clarity would get rid of a lot of work complexity. In a larger context, the employees may be told exactly what the organisation is trying to achieve during that year. And in that what exactly would be the role of the employee..... In a more specific context, the task of the employee on any working day in the year should be outlined.

Before you can write clearly, you have to be able to think clearly. A big reason why many writers don't see the desired success in conveying their message is that they were not focused on a clear message. Good writing usually stems directly from clear thinking.

The writing should be correctly planned and expressed in a logical way, and the writer should make sure that the ideas flow smoothly from the beginning to the end. The message must be so clear that even the most uninterested person in the world should readily understand it. The encoder must be absolutely clear about all the aspects of the central idea and about the purpose for which it is to be communicated. Next to it, he must be clear about the selection, suitability and usage of the medium.

The signals of the encoded message must be carefully composed and transmitted well. Clarity of written language is the first and foremost emphasis one should seek in writing. It can be achieved by writing to serve the purpose rather than to impress the readers. Understanding the subject first oneself brings about clarity in expression. Don't jump about from one part of the writing to another and then back to the first aspect. This is confusing for the reader. Deal with each aspect separately and clearly. Clear description brings the text alive, takes readers to where you have been and conjures up the right atmosphere. It can bring flavour in the most arid and dry news story and make the difference between a report that satisfies and one that does not.

Narrowing your scope and connecting a few topics to one thematic thread is essential to coherent writing. Too often, the writers feel they have to include everything they know about a topic or everything their committee discovered in its research. Either the writer wants to impress the reader, or the writer gathered pages of notes and feels the information has to fit somewhere. You should always gather much more material than you will need to write the e-mail, news release, or article, but that doesn't mean you should use it all.

Getting the meaning from your head *accurately* to the reader is the purpose of clarity.

Clarity of language is characterised by a number of qualities:

- The content is essential and self-evident. This means the words capture the most elementary features. Clarity comes, first and foremost, from identifying the essence of a story, the core of an idea, by formulating the executive summary of the story. That core might prompt wonder or disagreement, but there can be no doubt as to the meaning when a text is clear.

- The style of writing is simple. 'Simple' means using words or sentences which are easy to understand, particularly when there are more difficult alternatives. 'Simple' doesn't mean dumb or superficial. On the contrary, 'simplicity' means someone has penetrated the core of an issue and explained it with vision and conviction. Simplicity communicates, complexity confuses.
- The writing is frugal and economic. Few, not many words are used. This makes it easier for the readers to follow the thread of your story or the point of your argument. Frugality doesn't mean writing without flair or a personal style. It means allowing the readers to focus and make optimal use of their time and concentration. So, rather than inundating people with repartee, lengthy anecdotes, and detailed descriptions, keep it short and sweet!
- The text is constructed logically, with each level supporting the next. The paragraphs or chapters function as logical bridges to the next part of your story, in a way that takes your reader through your thoughts step-by-step. Remember, good structure creates clarity, and bad structure weakens clarity.
- The story flows. The sentences and paragraphs have a rhythm. Flow is a quality that is difficult to describe in words, it is almost a physical quality of language that is experienced rather than understood. What you should look for is whether there is harmony between the flow on the one hand and the content and structure on the other.

Editing is like sculpting: you start with a big slab of marble and chip away until the final shape emerges. Here you begin with your first draft (in writing or in a speech) and refine it ruthlessly, cut away superfluous which can be hard, considering all the blood, sweat and tears you have invested in it. Clarity, however, is achieved by getting rid of everything that is not essential and rewriting your text until you have found the best way to express something.

Clarity is best achieved during the editing phase because of the distance you put between yourself and the text when reviewing and rewriting it. This puts your writing in perspective and allows you to critically evaluate the strengths and weaknesses of your work. Clarity should be your guiding principle during the editing process to check whether the focus, purpose, meaning, substance and structure are self-evident.

How to achieve clarity?

- Choose precise, concrete and familiar words
- Construct effective sentences and paragraphs

Choose Precise, Concrete and Familiar Words

Clarity is achieved through a balance between precise language and familiar language

When you have the choice between a long word and a short word, choose the short familiar word

When in doubt, use the more familiar words; audience will understand them better. For example, use *pay* instead of remuneration and *invoice* instead of *statement of payment*

For example:

Unfamiliar – It is our endeavour to expedite the process of disseminating information by using optimum words in lieu of bombastic words so the meaning is not obfuscated.

Familiar - We will try to give information in simple words instead of complicated words so the meaning is not confusing.

Avoid technical terms and business jargon when the reader is not acquainted with them.

For example:

Unfamiliar – Assessed valuation

Familiar – Property value for tax purpose

Unfamiliar – You will receive reactivation and assistance consistent with your requirements.

Familiar – You will get the amount of help you need.

Construct Effective Sentences and Paragraphs:

Important characteristics: Length, Unity, Coherence and Emphasis

Length:

- Try for an average sentence length of 10 to 15 words.
- When the sentence length increases, try to cut it down to two sentences.
- If the sentences are too short, the resulting language becomes very choppy.

Unity:

- In a sentence, have one main idea.

- In case of other (two or more) ideas, they must be closely related.

For example: 'I enjoy a good movie and Mumbai is a very congested city' is obviously not a unified sentence.

Coherence:

- Words are arranged so that the ideas clearly express the intended meaning.
- Place the correct modifier as closely as possible to the word it is supposed to modify.
- In the examples that follow, notice that an 'unclear' sentence conveys the wrong meaning.

For example:

Unclear - Being an excellent vocalist, I am sure that you can sing this song.

Clear - Being an excellent vocalist, you can surely sing this song.

Or:

Unclear - His report was about managers, broken down by age and gender.

Clear - His report focused on age and gender of managers.

Emphasis:

- To give force to the important parts of sentences and paragraphs.
- Most often, put the main ideas upfront within a sentence.
- The writers must decide as to what needs emphasis, and then decide the correct sentence structure.

For example:

Little emphasis - The car finally crossed the speed limit, and it went out of control.

Better emphasis - As the car crossed the speed limit, it went out of control.

Or

Little emphasis - Candidates should be motivated and should have interest in dynamic and static testing of material, and have those prerequisites and others.

Better emphasis - The prerequisites in candidates should include expertise in dynamic and static testing of material.

You should be clear in your thoughts to begin with and know the essence of your communication; only then can you be clear in your writing. Think about the key points and how to put them in context, facts at your disposal and the most logical order of your message. Clarity again like concreteness can provide the recipient the most value in the least amount of time.

Plan out the presentation of your ideas from the beginning that is (a) acceptable to your audience, (b) encourages their interest, and (c) helps them track with you while they read on.

Courteousness

Hanuman has an orderly refinement in the speech that is remarkable, and he speaks gracious words that are pleasing. His purpose is to find out the reason why Ram and Lakshman were in the forest. However, he does not demand to know the reason, he requests for the information. He says, *"...It is indeed puzzling how you have reached this countryside!"*

"... Maybe you are powerful Gods in human form! Who exactly you might be?"

That is courtesy! The question *"Who are you and what are you doing here?"* is worded so differently that there is no trace of rudeness or arrogance in his query. The need for information is evident, but Hanuman is polite but firm. He does not wish to offend the strangers in the forest but still he surely wants to know the reason for their presence.

The need for courtesy has not changed even now. People now, as then, as always expect and deserve courtesy. Not just in business but also in everyday interactions, not just in written messages but also in verbal communication, courtesy can make or break a deal, can nurture or rupture a relationship.

In business, you deal with individuals, not machines. In both written and oral communication, you can be courteous and still be direct and business-oriented. Most people respond more readily to a positive interaction. Your ability to respect people can put them at ease and motivate them to respond likewise. Remember that your behaviour is observed and judged daily by the employers, clients and co-workers, and your ability to establish effective working relationships with others can affect your career.

In personal relationships, treating others with respect, kindness, and consideration creates meaningful friendships and leads to self-fulfilment.

Courteous communication not only takes into account the audience's reaction to your message but also their feelings. Just like consideration, it is important to understand your audience and their emotions as you craft your message.

To do this, put yourself in the other person's shoes. Think about the kind of service you want, that we all want. When we go into a shop, we want the salesperson to pay attention to us, to make us feel that our business is important. When we call or e-mail someone, we want that person to reply to our messages promptly. It is human nature to expect courtesy, so effective writers are courteous to their readers. As we have seen time after time, courtesy pays off.

Courtesy stems from a sincere you-attitude. It is not merely politeness with mechanical insertion of 'please' and 'thank you', although applying socially accepted manners is indeed a form of courtesy. Rather it is politeness that grows out of respect and concern for others. You should have it; if not, then try to have consideration for others.

Whether you are communicating verbally or in writing, with friends or business associates, the tone of your message needs to be right. The tone conveys a particular message from you as the writer and likewise affects the reader in a particular way. Consequently, it can also affect how the reader perceives the message you are communicating.

Trust is hard to earn and maintain in business relationships. Sometimes, something as seemingly small as a misunderstanding or perceived rudeness in business communication can wreck a working relationship. In business communication, good manners can mean the difference between a profit and a loss. Learning to be courteous and polite at all times can save wasted energy at work worrying about when you may have fumbled in business etiquette and courtesy.

Employees are particularly sensitive to discourteous communication from their superiors, such as the bosses who talk down to their subordinates, interrupt conversations or criticize the employees publicly when it could be done in private. Many employees see a failure to communicate company policy or planning as discourteous, reflecting a lack of respect for them

What is courteous communication?

Courteous communication is friendly, open and honest. There are no insults dressed as humour, or passive-aggressive tones. Complaints come out as sincere, grievances sound genuine without being accusatory. The message (written or oral) certainly expresses what the sender/encoder wants to convey, but there is evident respect and empathy for the receiver.

The sender of the message should be sincerely polite, thoughtful, insightful and enthusiastic. Courteous message has the following features:

- Courtesy implies taking into consideration the viewpoints and feelings of the receiver of the message.
- Courteous message is positive and focused on the audience.
- The language shows respect for the receiver.
- It is impartial and unbiased.

How to be courteous

- Be sincerely tactful, thoughtful and appreciative.
- Maintain the right tone in the communiqué.
- Use positive words, avoid negative words.
- Use expressions that show respect.
- Choose non-discriminatory expressions.

Be sincerely tactful, thoughtful and appreciative:

Tact:

Tact is basically saying negative things in a manner that does not offend. The oft-heard sentence, 'No offence meant, but…' does not figure in a courteous message. The intention to offend is evident in this preface. Sometimes this may seem as frankness to the sender or maybe the sender is trying to be concise! Maybe you are not happy with the situation and want to confront the culprit (in your opinion!). Whatever the matter, the basic courtesy can and should be maintained.

For example:

Tactless, blunt – 'The entire recording is off-tune!'

More tactful – 'The recording could be more harmonious!'

Tactless, Blunt – 'Don't break the queue, we are standing here in line!'

More Tactful – 'Maybe you did not see me, I too am in the queue!'

Thoughtfulness and Appreciation

People do work and there is generally no comment if the work is going on well. However, just one mistake/problem and the criticism – honest or otherwise – is prompt. The only time some seniors talk to their staff is when something is wrong! This is not right. If there is appreciation, then criticism too is taken well. You may feel that why show appreciation when the employees are doing what they are being paid for? But, just some gesture, a few words of acknowledgement would spur people to put in even better performance.

We all need to feel that people notice and appreciate our good efforts. This does not mean going overboard and praising someone all the time. But, for a task well done, for a service especially good, let them know that you appreciate their work. And let the person's supervisor know too.

These traits can become a habit and will help build goodwill.

Maintain the right tone

Using the appropriate tone in business writing is an important aspect of communicating the intended message to achieve the desired results. When determining the appropriate tone to use, ask yourself why you are writing the document (the purpose), who the audience is, and what you want them to learn and to do with the information in the document. When you know the answers to these questions, you will be able to identify and use the appropriate tone. In turn, the appropriate tone will help you to engage your readers and propel them to action.

The tone for most of the business writing should not be too casual, even though each company's culture is obviously somewhat distinct. Even when you know the readers quite well, and almost certainly when you do not, the tone should be quite formal in most of the written business communication. Job position also plays a part in this; you might use a slightly different tone with your colleagues than you do with your boss.

Though most business correspondence is fairly formal, do not make the mistake of being *too* formal.

Your tone should be courteous and professional at all times, and it should convey strength and confidence. When you use a confident and courteous tone, the readers are more likely to agree and accept the message you are conveying. However, you must not be curt, overconfident, or arrogant, as this may alienate your reader. If you are too tentative, the readers might not take you seriously, but if you are too demanding, they might resent your request and are less inclined to comply. Thus, it is important to find the proper balance.

Be honest and sincere. Most of the readers can discern when someone is taking liberties with honesty. If they believe in what you say, you will accomplish more and build more trust.

In some cases, especially when you are upset, you may need to give yourself some time before you respond so that you can be objective; don't write when you're overly emotional.

Here are some examples of the right tone to use in particular kinds of business writing.

- Awarding a promotion - appreciative, enthusiastic
- Applying for a job position - enthusiastic, confident
- Denying a request - regretful, courteous
- Rejecting a job applicant - thankful, regretful
- Declining a job offer - appreciative, regretful
- Apologizing to a customer for a mistake - humble, appreciative to the person for being a client, confident that the mistake will be remedied
- Apologizing to a customer; unable to correct the mistake - humble, appreciative, regretful that the mistake cannot be remedied
- Reprimanding an employee - firm but courteous (address the issue; don't attack the individual)

Use positive words, avoid negative expressions

If you want a positive response to your memo or report, then do not use negative words. Some negative words to avoid in writing are: cannot, damage, do not, error, fail, impossible, little value, loss, mistake, not, problem, refuse, stop, unable to, and unfortunately.

Your aim of writing needs to be the solution, not the problem. All communication needs to sound collaborative and positive, and instructions need to be clear and tell the reader what to do, rather than what not to do. Positive words to use include: benefit, it is best to, issue, matter, progress, success, fortunate, and valuable.

Use expressions that show respect

Re-read the message after writing and see if you would like to receive such a message, does it make you feel good or are you offended? No reader would want a message that is offensive. Are there any expressions that many find irritating? Here are some:

- Contrary to your inference
- I do not agree with you
- If you care
- I am sure you must realize

Along with irritating expressions, questionable humour too is not good. Sometimes what you may find funny may be distasteful to another person. Why take a chance at being offensive?

Choose non-discriminatory expressions

More and more these days, sexist terms are frowned at. Try to stick to 'person' and use both her/him wherever needed. Nowadays the terms 'they, their, them…' are used even in singular. Be fully aware of gender, race, age, colour, creed or ethnic origins. Omit expressions that could hurt, belittle or irritate somebody.

Hanuman and Sita's First Meeting: Establish Trust

Hanuman was well aware that he might not be taken at face value. He would certainly have to establish his authenticity. He had no recourse to anything else except his speech. So he used his speech most effectively by first talking about a subject dear to Sita's heart ... Shri Ram. Hanuman praised Ram and gave a few details of his father and brothers. This initially seemed enough to convince Sita but soon doubts assailed her. So, once again Hanuman gave a few more details and narrated the whole episode of Sita's abduction – information that a disguised rakshas would not have access to. This time he gained her full confidence.

Lessons:

The first meeting is crucial! Whether it is with business associates or people in a social group, it is important to create a believable first impression. Here we need to remember three points.

First is the subject! In a business environment, it is not difficult to choose a topic. It would definitely be the common business interests, the latest shared concerns and mutually beneficial issues. It would be a good idea to initially reveal only part of the information to gauge if others are interested. Once the concern and participation of the other members are established, only then can more material be shared.

In case of a social group too subjects of common interest need to be tackled to begin with. If you join an obviously classical music-loving group of people (say in a party), would you suddenly start discussing a cricket game? (Cricket is a national pastime in India, so who knows!) Maybe not a good idea! However, if you too are a classical music aficionado, then it is easy to mingle in. If you are a maestro or a connoisseur, then it is even easier. But wait; do not show off your mastery over the subject immediately. Know-alls generally are put-offs. Not just in case of music, but any topic. So, participate in the conversation with interesting comments or informative observations. Let your knowledge show gradually. Keep something back, to keep others' interest alive.

The second point is to judge the other party's interest. Here one has to be very careful, especially in business meetings. You don't want to give offence; you don't want to seem like a snoop, you don't want to worry the others about your intention. So, proceed with caution. Share just a little information to understand if you are on the same page. Once their integrity is established, you can take the association further.

The issue of the other party's integrity does not carry so much weight in social interactions. Yes, you should not give all your history to strangers unless you are sure of their intentions. Here too the same adage applies - proceed with caution!

The third point is the evidence or proof. Don't show all the cards unless you are convinced about the other person. Keep some substantial benefit or advantage in reserve. Offering everything right in the initial stages might be risky. It could be taken as eagerness on your part, or even desperation. Keep such stuff for the time when your and the other party's credibility is established in each other's view. Then the benefit on offer will have more weight.

Hanuman and Ravan's first meeting: Grab attention

Hanuman knew that a complete verbal onslaught on Ravan and his misdeeds would not go down well with the rakshas assembly. Neither would extensive praise of

Ram be appreciated nor would threats against Lanka be received quietly. So, taking a conciliatory tone initially, he, later on, launches into full-fledged denouncement of Ravan and prediction about the destruction of the rakshasas and Ravan's end. By this time, the audience is listening to him fully focussed.

Lessons:

There are some announcements that are unpalatable to the listeners; some important news that could begin mayhem if told directly! At such times, give the audience what they want to hear in the beginning, but keep it relevant to the topic in hand. Once their attention is grabbed, then come out with what you really want to say.

For example, let us assume that you have to declare a 'no-bonus' year in the General Body Meeting. This is bound to create pandemonium and anything you want to say further will be drowned in the ensuing melee. Maybe you could begin by taking stock of the company's financial situation, external factors and immediate measures proposed. This need not be a long introduction, but only to seize the attention of the assembly. Once that is done, you talk about the 'no-bonus' situation and any positive measures taken to improve the situation.

This kind of communication does not apply to the crisis situations. At those times, it is better to be direct and quick, as we shall see in the next example when Hanuman meets Bharat in Nandigram.

Hanuman and Bharat's first meeting: Critical news instantly

Hanuman knew that right at that moment, Bharat would not be in a frame of mind to listen to the lengthy narratives about the happenings. All that he would be interested in knowing was if and when was his beloved Ram to return. In fact, as 14 years of Ram's exile are over and there is no news from Ram, Bharat is planning to enter the fire to end his life. It is really imperative that Bharat learns about Ram's eminent arrival. So, Hanuman tells him that and then the rest of the saga.

In fact, while narrating the happenings, Hanuman very prudently omits the mention of Sita's fire ordeal. He did not want to offend the sensibilities of the already suffering Bharat. Or maybe he did not wish Bharat to misinterpret Ram's action.

Lessons:

When there is a crisis situation, it is always best to give critical information right in the beginning that will put the audience's minds at rest. Later on, the details can be given as required. This is quite evident post surgical procedures when all that the patient's relatives wish to know is the success or otherwise of the operation.

Hanuman disagrees with the monkey leaders: Analysis and logic

This is a fantastic piece of oratory that shows excellent analytical power and logic. One by one, Hanuman negated the monkey generals' views as well as Jambuvant's. His arguments are irrefutable and true. What can we learn from this? Proper analysis of a situation leads to logical conclusions.

❐

Tapaswini Sulabha's Proper Speech

Sulabha's advice on proper speech is as valid today as it was during the time Mahabharat was written. Let us try to understand how we can benefit from this counsel that Sulabha gave king Janak.

To begin with, let us look at the five characteristics of speech These are:

1. Ambiguity
2. Ascertainment
3. Priority
4. Analysis
5. Bias

Ambiguity

Ambiguity is one of the most common problems in speech or writing. A word, phrase or sentence is ambiguous if it has more than one meaning. When you use such words or phrases in your speech, the exact meaning may not be clear. Some words such as light, bear, note, over, etc. are examples of ambiguous words in everyday use.

When you say, *"Seema cannot bear children."*, what exactly do you mean? That Seema cannot stand to be around children or she cannot have children of her own.

Another type of ambiguity is when a sentence is made in such a way that it can have more than one underlying structure. For example, *"Visiting relatives can be boring."* So what is boring? Is it the relatives who are visiting or the act of going over to the relatives for a visit?

Some interesting examples of ambiguity are:

- I will bring my bike tomorrow if it looks nice in the morning.
- In a restaurant: Please wait for the hostess to be seated.
- Students hate annoying professors.
- Happily they left.

And the oft-quoted example is of R.D. Jones and his Sewing Machine:

The following is an advertisement from a real-life newspaper, which appeared four days in a row – the last three hopelessly trying to correct the first day's mistake.

Monday: For sale: R.D. Jones has one sewing machine for sale. Phone 948-0707 after 7 P.M. and ask for Mrs. Kelly, who lives with him cheap.

Tuesday: Notice: We regret having erred in R.D. Jones' ad yesterday. It should have read: 'One sewing machine for sale cheap. Phone 948-0707 and ask for Mrs. Kelly, who lives with him after 7 P.M.'

Wednesday: Notice: R.D. Jones has informed us that he has received several annoying telephone calls because of the error we made in the classified ad yesterday. The ad stands correct as follows: 'For sale – R.D. Jones has one sewing machine for sale. Cheap. Phone 948-0707 after 7 P.M. and ask for Mrs. Kelly, who lives with him.'

Thursday: Notice: I, R.D. Jones, have no sewing machine for sale. I intentionally broke it. Don't call 948-0707 as I have had the phone disconnected. I have not been carrying on with Mrs. Kelly. Until yesterday, she was my housekeeper, but she has now quit.

Ascertainment

In a speech or in written text, the meaning of some words or sentences can be taken in different ways. These meanings can be contradictory. The correct meaning needs to be ascertained by weighing probabilities and reasons. It also depends on the context. This is known as Sankhya.

Let me illustrate this with two variations of a well-known quote. These are:

- It is lonely at the top…and cold.
- It is lonely at the top but I surely like the view.

Most of us know what this quote alludes to! It is certainly lonely and cold on any mountaintop, as also the view from there would be great. So does this quote refer to view from a mountaintop? Of course, not you would insist. This is about successful persons or leaders who have reached the top position.

We know this because we are aware of the premise of the quote. We know that getting to the top does take a tremendous amount of effort, skills, and a lot of self-made luck... but once at the top, it is a very lonely place. Maybe because the desperation to put forward the best image puts pressure to share honestly or reveal faults. Maybe the top honchos start feeling too impressed with themselves to connect with those beneath them. Conversely, those beneath them begin to treat the boss as though they are on a pedestal. Such painful mindset also seems to isolate those who excel in other areas.

So, we have drawn a conclusion about being lonely at the top based on our understanding of the context and no lonely mountaintop figures anywhere in our conclusion.

Priority

Sentence structure, or syntax, is about the relationships among the words that form a sentence. It is one of the most important factors affecting the readability of a text. In fact, one readability study has shown that improvements to the sentence structure generally have a greater impact on the readability than the elimination of obscure terminology. If it is easy to understand how the words of a sentence relate to each other, the readers are often able to figure out the meaning of unfamiliar words.

In English, the usual order of ideas is subject – verb – object. The grammar and the intended meaning would dictate the order of words. Sometimes, the grammar may be right but the meaning may not be conveyed. Have a look:

"Colourless green ideas sleep furiously."

Linguist Noam Chomsky created this sentence – which is grammatically correct but incomprehensible – to demonstrate that the rules governing syntax are distinct from the meanings the words convey.

A sentence structure has two aspects:

Complexity (including length); and

Organization (word order).

Both these aspects are related to each other because the word order is the principal device available in English or in any language, to express the interrelationship of ideas in a sentence. The more ideas a sentence contains (complexity), the greater the temptation to depart from the way the sentences are normally organized in order to make it clear how the ideas relate to each other.

Weighing the relative strength or weakness of the faults or merits (ascertained by the above process), consists in ensuring the accuracy of the order of the words employed in a sentence. In a speech or a presentation, in an argument or a chat when we talk, we definitely would do better to put forward the most relevant point first, followed by the points of less importance.

The meaning of sentences depends on more than the meaning of the individual words they contain. It also depends on the relationships among the ideas conveyed by the words. The order in which these ideas are presented, greatly affects the ease with which they are understood.

Ideas don't make much sense if they are not arranged in some way. Something has to come first, something has to go last, and several things usually end up in the middle, one after another, in a logical order. To determine that order, think of a speech as being divided into parts, one for each group of ideas the writer is working with. To come up with a beginning, think about the best way to introduce these groups of ideas so that the readers will be interested in them and want to find out more. Then, arrange the groups so that each one leads naturally into the next in a way that is interesting, entertaining and consistent with the reader's expectations. Finally, come up with an ending that feels finished and gives the reader something to think about.

Every piece can be separated into parts where each part contains a group of ideas that go together. The trick is to put the parts in the best order so that the reader/listener is entertained and able to understand how each part relates to the next and how all parts relate to the piece as a whole. To figure this out, it's helpful to name the different parts of a piece.

For example, for an e-mail informing about a conference, you would first mention the subject of the conference, then the speakers, venue, timing, etc.

If you wish to send a mail to your friends to invite them for dinner, the date might come first, then the timing, assuming it is at your residence.

Analysis

In written or oral communication, an analysis of the meaning of a sentence is important. A statement can be influenced by the word order:

Did he say who he was?

Who did he say he was?

In relation with the words, the structure of the sentence also depends on the individual meaning of the words or word-groups making up the sentence. Depending on the context and our understanding of the nuances of the language, we come to the right meaning. For example:

Shankar likes Rekha more than Sheila. - So, does Shankar like Rekha more than he likes Sheila or does Shankar like Rekha more than Sheila likes Rekha?

Only through the context in which these sentences appear can we know which of the two possible meanings is intended.

Meaning of a word cannot be simply gained by consulting the dictionary, because the dictionary definitions of a word are 'context-free'. That is the reason behind the query – 'Do you mean funny, peculiar, or funny, ha ha?' when someone says 'its funny!'

Every word has a direct meaning called the denotative meaning. In addition, the words also acquire implied meanings called connotative meanings. Connotations are understood based only on an individual's experience. If the encoder and decoder do not share the same connotative meaning for a word, miscommunication can occur.

If the receiver does not understand the connotation attributed by the sender, miscommunication takes place. But when words are used for denotations alone, not much damage will be done. To overcome this barrier to communication, the communicator should choose the precise and exact word that will carry the same meaning for the receiver in the given context. The meaning of the word is related to context at the connotational level. A complimentary expression may derive a connotative derogative meaning that will ruin the communication process.

If you examine the word 'fellow', you will find so many connotations to it. The word used with adjectives such as 'nice' and 'lousy' change the complexion of the word 'fellow'. A 'nice fellow' and a 'lousy fellow' are poles apart. If you call someone a 'fellow scholar', he is your contemporary. Fellowship simply means companionship or friendliness. However, in special contexts, it can have different connotations. You can be a scholar with UGC (University Grants Commission) getting a fellowship.

After analysing a statement, it should stand the test of understanding on the connotative level for the intended audience. The encoder, thus, needs to be aware of this point.

Bias

Bias is a particular tendency or inclination, especially the one that prevents unprejudiced consideration of a question. It means slanted, one-sided, prejudiced, predisposed, and dogmatic opinion. In writing or speech, it is not considered proper to show your bias. This bias can be of many types. Here are some guidelines to avoid bias:

- Race bias is absolutely not right. Moreover, the terms once considered to be accurate or acceptable may be considered offensive today. When referring to a group of people, use the term that the group currently uses to refer to themselves.
- Gender bias also should be guarded against. Sometimes, it is convenient to use plural in place of gender specific term. However, at other times that becomes tortuous. Nowadays, it is accepted to use the female-specific pronouns unless you are talking about the male gender particularly.
- Another kind of bias is a strong opinion about something. It is based more on feelings and opinions than on facts or maybe on a person's past experiences. You can be biased in favour of something or against it.
- Sometimes, bias can be intentional and you would use it to convince someone about something. At other times, it could be unintentional, probably a result of incomplete information.
- Perceptual bias is the lens we automatically filter all of our experiences through. It makes some things seem more noteworthy than others. It guides our reactions and thoughts about what we experience, see, or feel. You cannot get entirely away from perceptual bias.

Who you are, where you come from, and what you have experienced before, all create that bias of perception in your mind.

It is really not possible to guard against all the biases, but if you do and succeed then that is brilliant. You should strive for it!

Features of Fitting Speech

What qualities should our speech have?

- Sensible, precise and logical.
- Not unnecessarily meandering or repetitive.
- Smooth, sure and sweet.
- Modest, true and refined.
- Not elliptical or imperfect.
- Thoughtful and easy to comprehend.
- Characterised by proper order and consistent with one another.

Any speech should not be triggered by desire or wrath or fear or cupidity or abjectness or deceit or shame or compassion or pride.

The speaker, the listener and the spoken words should be compliant with one another. If the speaker either speaks without a thought to the listener or alternatively speaks only to please the listener, then the words can be misleading or erroneous. Speaker should employ words that are, while expressing his own meaning, intelligible to the hearer as well, only then the speech has meaning.

❐

Part-II

LET'S TALK BUSINESS!

Corporate Scenario

Change is continual. In this ICE age - Information, Communication, Education - the speed of change is faster than ever before. The driving force behind this phenomenon is the revolution in the field of communication. The turning point was when an effective communications satellite was sent up above the earth for the first time that made possible instantaneous communication from one part of the world to another. The consequence of the communication revolution is that the technology that is also developing at superfast speed is spreading globally at the blink of an eye. The same technology is available with little difference to competing organisations.

Communication is no longer just one-to-one activity over telephones or mobile phones. Internet has changed the way people communicate. Communication can be managed much more easily now. Everybody can access or distribute information speedily and widely almost without cost. For organisations, this translates as their employees can keep up with what is happening in the field, they can seek other opportunities and move on.

The customer base too has expanded as the international arena has opened up. The competition is global and relentless. To keep up, the players have had to learn a whole new set of rules and techniques. The geographical borders have blurred and the clock-watchers and the timekeepers have become extinct. The time-differences between the organisations' locations and the customers' locations necessitate work round the clock.

The intangible assets, knowledge or skill sets are precious and cannot be the property of the organisation. The knowledge can be stored and managed but it depends on the employees. They may decide not to share the acquired knowledge. This makes communication even more important. To evolve and progress, the companies have to develop their own survival strategies, which are necessarily based on knowledge and communication.

To sum up, the balance of power between the employer and the individual employee has changed. Employees are more visible; they have more ability to move; they are more aware of their rights. Also the organisations are not able to control as much of consumers' lives as they used to. The seller's market no longer is valid. Consumers can easily move from one supplier to another.

Corporates have to develop some kind of framework to accommodate these changes and, at the same time, build a strong organisation that is profitable - an organisation, that keeps its employees loyal, proud and making significant contributions towards its goal.

How to achieve this state of continuity during change? Here too communication is the key.

The purpose of 'Communication during Change' is to establish timely communication across the organisation and to prepare the employees with skill sets to respond to changes in real time. These simple goals cover a myriad of communication processes that include top to down, down to top and lateral communication. As today's organisations are in a perpetual state of flux, the entire communication has to be geared to such a state of affairs.

For 'Communication during Change, organisations need to adopt a three-layered Corporate Communications Strategy.

The first level focuses on organisation-wide communication, where loyalty and pride to the organisation need to be instilled in each employee.

The second level is the actual communication about change.

The third level is day-to-day work communication.

❒

The First Level

Organisational pride and loyalty – Lessons from Military Leadership

It was during the 1971 war, an incident took place that illustrates more than anything else the kind of loyalty that an officer of the Indian Army inspires. This incident took place in the Western sector. For here the fighting was particularly bitter with many lives lost on both sides. Many units crossed the enemy lines easily enough, though they got bogged down in minefields. The enemy launched a series of counter-attacks headed by tanks of an Armoured Brigade. Some units suffered huge losses in the concentrated artillery fire and aerial bombing. One Indian battalion had its commanding officer shot by the enemy fire. The counter-attack was eventually stopped by sheer grit and determination.

When this officer was hit in the leg, he was lying in a trench. When his soldier saw him, he ran to him disregarding the bullets flying all around him. The officer shouted for the soldier to go back to his trench. Regardless, he continued to move on and lifting the officer, who could not now walk on his shoulders, he ran back to safety.

"Why are you doing this? Save your life, go on", shouted the officer.

"I will save my life Sir and also yours", was the response.

"Both of us could be killed."

"It is all right, Sir, if I do not save you, who will?"

Finally both, the officer and the saviour soldier, came back from the war alive.

What made the soldier risk his own life to save his superior officer's life? What is it that prompts such behaviour? Nobody would have blamed the soldier had he tried to save his life and run away. But he did not. Was it loyalty? Was it pride in his own army unit - the soldiers and officers of this unit are not cowards? Was it a wish for an award - but seriously while bullets are flying all around you, how could anyone think about the later awards? Or was it the fact that the officer led from the front? Or the soldier knew that if he did not help the officer, there was nobody in the world who could have saved him! Maybe he felt responsible for his officer's life.

To understand the military mind-set, let us see how they function.

Through time immemorial, the Indian Army has lived up to a golden tradition of valour, heroism, compassion, sacrifice and fortitude. Its soldiers are amongst the best in the world, a classic example of unity in diversity. The greatest binding force in the Indian Army remains unit cohesion, tradition and the proverbial 'izzat' or honour of their unit or Regiment. Truly unique is their pride in unit identification, and traditions handed down through ages. All these form the bedrock of 'Ethos'.

The service ethos as a whole is the main reason for such loyalty. It revolves around the central pivot of 'discipline' - do what you are told! The hierarchical structure coupled with the discipline ensures obedience. Of course, blind obedience is not a good practice. Intelligent obedience, even if it means physical discomfort, subordination of own will to that of mission's needs, trust in the establishment or superiors, complete faith that they have your larger interest at heart though only next to that of mission accomplishment needs.

This loyalty is developed over the years and does not come by in a short time. This is so because motivation drives the men to accomplish what may seem impossible. Motivation comes only after mutual trust is established between the leader and the led which takes time, expensive training, field experience, the ups and downs of operational experience, mission.

Why it is that services display loyalty towards their service (organisation) in a measure much greater than what is visible in other organisations?

The reasons are many:

1. Clear, unambiguous mission statement
2. Family welfare
3. Esprit de corps
4. Leading by example

Mission above all

Loyalty towards organisation is simply translated in a single phrase – 'mission accomplished'. It presupposes that missions themselves are undoubtedly set correctly by the superiors for their subordinates. While setting a mission, the superiors take into account the task set by *their* superiors and the prevalent circumstances which are: environment, resources, threats, strengths and the likely pay-offs. Often the critics argue later after the mission that the tasks set were incorrect. That is purely hindsight. And that kind of logic is not considered at all.

The Mission

'Mission' is a complete word which can have different connotations at different levels of hierarchy. At the grassroots level, the mission may either be a simple task or a difficult one. For example, check, identify and permit entry or gift-wrap an article purchased. At higher levels of hierarchy, it could be to capture a piece of territory or for top management, it can be to achieve a turnover of 1,000 crores. For the government, it could be to rid the country of malaria, hepatitis in five years or achieve a goal of self-sufficiency in food-items in *x* years.

Clearly spelling out a mission is a very critical task. Only a confused leader can give a fuzzy task. In the armed forces, one of the main reasons of success and loyalty of subordinates is due to clear spelling out of the mission. Generally, a mission statement is specific and stands still till it is achieved or modified duc to the changed environment.

In the armed forces, mission statements are carefully worded and form the very basis of all the activities. That helps to a large extent in co-ordinated action by many agencies, which binds the rank and file leading to a cohesive force, which is loyal to the organisation.

Wherever the mission statement is erroneous, ambiguous or fuzzy, disaster is bound to result.

Loyalty

Loyalty is a very difficult word to define and understand. It is often mistaken for towing the superior's line or being overtly helpful to the personal needs of the superiors, or in another totally different manner, being overzealous of the comforts of the subordinates without caring for the success of the mission. All these are not only aberrations of loyalty but are grossly out of phase with what loyalty really means.

Loyalty to a superior is only with respect to fulfilling her wishes and cooperating with her so long as these directly meet the needs of fulfilling the mission. The training, education and discerning intellect is enough to judge whether the actions demanded from us by the superiors are in consonance with the fulfilment of the mission. No great debate or brainstorming is required for this. Even the lowest worker knows in his/her heart or brain whether the senior is doing whatever is required for the mission's success or his own limited benefits.

Family Welfare

A soldier while on duty or a mission does not have to worry about his family's welfare. He has complete confidence that the organisation (the Army, Navy or Air Force) will look after his family and take care of all the problems or eventualities. There is family pension, medical assistance, schools for the children, where admissions are ensured, and professional colleges for the children of the servicemen.

Esprit de corps

A feeling of camaraderie or esprit de corps prevalent in the forces is something unique. The unit is like a close-knit family. Even after retirement, this feeling persists. The capacity of people to maintain belief in the institution or the goal or even in oneself and others marks the uniqueness of the services. Though this term applies particularly to military personnel and to the members of the sports teams, it is also applicable in business and in any other organisational context, particularly in times of stress or controversy. While the term is often used by authority figures as a generic value judgement of the will-power, obedience and self-discipline of a group tasked with performing duties assigned by a superior, more accurately it refers to the level of individual faith in the collective benefit gained by such performance.

For greater precision, it would be appropriate to distinguish two meanings of this expression, 'esprit de corps': a broad and a narrow sense. In a narrow sense, esprit de corps is a spirit of solidarity animating all the members of the same professional group. In a broader sense, the expression 'esprit de corps' designates the spirit of solidarity in general, not only in the professional group, but also in all those social circles (whatever they might be, such as class, caste, sect, etc.), in which the individual feels himself to be more or less subordinated to the interests of the group.

Historically, elite military units, such as special operations forces have 'high morale' due to both their training and pride in their unit.

Despite the intangible nature of morale, improvements in material factors (such as remuneration, food and shelter) can and does improve morale. However, history is filled with stories of the self-will and determination of a poorly supplied army maintaining morale to the very end. Here is one such inspiring example.

When the Siachen conflict began in 1984, the Indian army deployed on the high altitude glacier did not have any real awareness of the extreme weather conditions. The Siachen glacier is one of the world's most inhospitable terrains. It is a frozen river of ice with temperatures ranging from -35° Celsius in summer to -60° Celsius in winter. Add to it unseen crevasses, avalanches and howling winds and it has all the appearances of hell. Poorly equipped to deal with such inclement weather and barely outfitted even to survive in the cold environment, it successfully repelled two probes by the enemy troops in June 1984.

Gasping for air at those altitudes, troops had to claw their way up using ropes, ladders, ice axes and pitons, and, thereafter, endeavour to push hard to dislodge the enemy. Many such attempts made by the enemy were successfully repulsed by the unsuitably equipped Indian troops. Severe cold would jam weapons and frostbites would make men writhe in pain. But the morale stayed high and the men kept winning!

Dress

Outward bearing is the first index of discipline and esprit de corps. Officers and men realise that they carry the badge of their regiment, and that those who see them look on them not as individuals but as the representatives of their regiment.

Every officer must, therefore, carry himself erect, and see that his uniform is clean and in good condition, and that it is worn correctly. Until he is satisfied that his own turnout is correct, he cannot expect a high standard from those under his command.

Men can look smart in battle dress, if it is worn correctly and the necessary trouble is taken; alternatively, a slovenly man can carry it in such a fashion that he looks little better than a tramp. Here again the responsibility lies with the officer and the N.C.O. If they themselves are smartly turned out, the more enterprising men will take their cue from them and the rest will need little encouragement to follow their example.

Saluting

Saluting is reputed to date from the days of armour, the salute representing the motions of a knight raising the visor of his helmet with the open hand to the front, showing that, though raised, it contained no missile. The practice of giving 'eyes right' originated from the medieval days when it was the privilege of men at arms to look their superiors in the face, while others must pass with downcast eyes. The salute, therefore, is no sign of subservience: it is recognition of comradeship and mutual trust between men at arms. It is, at the same time, an acknowledgement of discipline, and a visible indication of the common obedience that all ranks owe to the nation and its service. Saluting is, thus, another indication of the esprit de corps and discipline of a unit.

The officer saluted must understand that it is his duty not only to acknowledge the salute but also to return it in a proper manner. He does so by saluting in the same way as the soldier, and not with the flick of a finger or the wave of his stick; nor does he return a salute with a cigarette in his mouth. When returning a salute, he should look the man in the face so that the man gains the impression that his quality as a soldier is being appraised. He should also take a deliberate note of the badge the man is wearing.

It is the duty of every officer not only to return salutes but also to see that he is properly saluted by those who should do so. Failure to salute is often due to shyness; or a man may think that he has not been noticed. An officer, who salutes others, who is confident of being saluted himself, and who intends to return salutes properly, will rarely find it necessary to check a man.

Drill and Physical Fitness

The above comments largely have reference to the development of esprit de corps by example. In this aspect, esprit de corps is hardly to be distinguished from the spirit of good discipline, and for its direct development, there is no surer method than regular spells of steady drill. Drill in this context is not meant to imply tedious parade ground movements carried out in a mechanical manner, but the physical satisfaction to be derived from sinking one's individuality in the perfect timing of a mass movement, in which every individual is keyed up to the maximum personal tension. Thus, this form of discipline is something more than blind and unquestioning obedience to orders: it is a rhythmic and automatic surging of the cohesive spirit of a body of men in times of crisis, so that all can draw on the common fund of courage and endurance.

Only the exceptional individual can face alone the onslaught of a massive enemy; but a man of even less than average courage can be counted on not to let down his stouter comrades if he has been trained in the discipline of mind and body. Such powers of endurance will be assisted by a high standard of physical fitness. In the earliest stages of their training, the troops are hardened by imposing severe tests on their physical stamina. They are made to march hard and far, in correct fashion, and, over short periods, to live hard. Other training is wasted on a man who crumples under the first test of physical endurance. No matter what the degree of an army's mechanization or motorization, it will never win its battles if its soldiers are 'soft'. Nor do these demands for the highest possible standard of discipline and physical fitness apply exclusively to the fighting arms. In modern war, any unit of any arm is likely to be called upon, at any moment, to assume a fighting role.

Leading by example

Leaders help themselves and others to do the right things. They set direction, build an inspiring vision, and create something new. Leadership is about mapping out where you need to go to 'win' as a team or an organisation. Leadership is dynamic, vibrant and inspiring.

Yet, while the leaders set the direction, they must also use management skills to guide their team to the right destination in a smooth and efficient way.

The army officers need to be the leaders and managers, both. The army training plays a big role in making leaders out of officers. There are some basic rules and tenets that are outlined during officer training. These help the officers to learn about leadership. Here are some interesting doctrines that hold universally true for a leader.

General

1. What do your men know about the organisation and the equipment of the Army and the men they are against?
2. What do your men know about:
   I. The reason for the conflict?
   II. Aims of the enemy?
   III. How enemy victory would affect the man in the street, e.g., his standard of living, the security of his family, his freedom of action and thought?
   IV. The general strategic situation?
3. How many of your men do you know by name, and what do you know of their characters?
4. Are you satisfied that your men will come to you with their complaints and troubles, because they realise that they will get a sympathetic hearing and good advice?

5. Are all ranks getting adequate recreational facilities?
6. What games do you play with your men?
7. Are you and all under your command physically fit and hard? If not, why not, and what are you going to do about it? Do you know which of your men have been in hospital recently, and whether they are really fit now?
8. Do you regularly go round to your men's dining halls at mealtimes, apart from your routine visit as an orderly officer?
9. What are the arrangements made for washing and personal hygiene? Are the men's arrangements as good as your own?
10. When were your men last on leave? If any of them were 'unlucky', what have you done about it?
11. Which of your men are doing more work than the rest? Are you making too much use of the willing, and allowing the lazy man to slack?
12. How are the men paid at home and in the field?
13. Do you know of the things a man's kit should consist? What have you done if a man is short of kit?
14. Are you satisfied that all your N.C.O.s are pulling their weight? If not, what have you done about it?
15. What steps have you taken to ensure that your sub-unit can carry on in the event of your becoming a casualty?
16. How many N.C.O.s have you trained to carry out the duties of one rank above their own?
17. Are you trying to make yourself competent to take over the job of the next senior man to you?

18. When did you last demonstrate or get the medical officer to show how to use a field dressing?
19. Have you explained to your men the objects of the various phases of training you have carried out?
20. Do you organise your training programme so that all men on parade are usefully employed – or are many of them for a greater part of the time merely spectators?
21. Will your headquarters be functioning efficiently and smoothly by the time your collective training starts?
22. What map-reading competitions have you held? Can you memorize a map for use at night?
23. What exercises have you carried out to ensure that your men are capable of keeping direction by day or by night, or in fog?
24. What are the advantages during training of beginning night operations an hour before dawn?
25. Who in your unit is detailed to reconnoitre and layout routes when moving into bivouac or occupying a defensive position?
26. What military inter-sub-unit competitions have you held during the past month? What were the views of your men on these competitions?
27. Have you fixed up a road model to teach your drivers traffic control and traffic discipline?
28. Have you made any attempt to improvise training equipment?
29. Why is camouflage done late more dangerous than no camouflage at all?

30. Do you discuss difficulties and compare notes with your fellow officers? Do you pass on tips, and consider theirs? When did you last display a piece of initiative? Have you ever volunteered an original idea on training or administration and secured its adoption?
31. Do you appreciate the fact that the instructions contained in each Army Training Memorandum apply to you personally, whatever your rank, and that it is your job to take action accordingly? Do you realise that it is your responsibility to read each Army Training Memorandum in its entirety - and not merely the paragraphs directed to your own arm?

Example is Everything

No exceptional measures should be necessary to instil this fighting spirit. If troops are well disciplined and physically fit, well trained in the use of their weapons, and satisfied that they have a very necessary job of work in hand for their country, they will fight bravely.

Nevertheless, the sternest test of discipline must always be reserved for the leader - the officer. In battle, example is everything. One determined officer can sway the fortunes of a whole front. The test is of self-discipline; and the ability to stand up to it can come only through the officer's personal resolve never to falter in the face of the enemy, and to see that he and his troops carry out their allotted tasks, no matter what is happening to the left, to the right, or in rear of them. Men who are well led will never fail even though their leader may be killed.

The Hero

For an officer or leader, who carries out this resolve, the maintenance of esprit de corps and discipline will not be difficult, for his efforts will be reinforced by hero worship. Few men are too 'superior' to have their heroes, and the moment a hero emerges, conduct ceases to be passive and becomes an active and positive urge to do what the hero does or the kind of things he would approve. One of the most significant services that a dominant leader ever renders to a body of men is to provide its members with a hero.

The Indian Army has great traditions and, under the inspiration of good leadership, it will know how to fight. The future of this growing Army largely depends on the junior leader. His responsibilities are heavy; but we have proved in the past that we have the right breed. At the present time, no better advice can be given to him than this – *Know your men and care for them. Go in with your men, lead them, and fight. Stick to your men, and fight on. Never give in, and never look over your shoulder.*

Lessons from the Military Adapted to the Corporate World

When the corporates wish to instil military-like loyalty amongst their employees, their management has to first cultivate 'officer-like' qualities. Let us see again what makes the military leadership so effective that the men are ready to lay down their lives for their cause.

1. Clear, unambiguous mission
2. Family welfare
3. Esprit de corps
4. Leading by example

Of course, one cannot compare military and corporate; the fundamental difference being that corporates exist to make profits. They are fully commercial organisations unlike the military, where this angle is completely absent. Notwithstanding this, there are still many military practices that are worth emulating. These practices will make a difference.

Clear mission

When the mission is clear and unambiguous, and each person knows his/her role towards accomplishing the mission, the time available for this, it is easy for the employee to plan the tasks.

Clearly spelling out a mission is a very critical task. Yet more often than not, this aspect is treated in a shallow manner. *"We will tell you as we go along!"* is the general attitude that can hinder a smooth course towards the mission. There should be a specific mission statement that should stand still till it is achieved or modified due to changed environment. Mission statements should be carefully worded and should form the very basis of all the activities. This would go a long way in a co-ordinated action by many departments in the organisation. This will bind the rank and file leading to a cohesive force, which is loyal to the organisation.

'Mission statement' here does not mean the company mission statement! It means the target or objective of a particular project or assignment. It is the 'deliverables' signifying a report or item that must be completed and delivered under the terms of an agreement or contract.

Now, the mission has to be accomplished through the employees and their welfare should be taken into consideration. This concern for the welfare of the employees is only because it is the physically and psychologically sound people, who can accomplish the mission quickly and completely.

Workplace events play a large part in changing employee morale, such as heavy layoffs, the cancellation of overtime, cancelling the benefit programs, and the lack of union representation. Other events can also influence the workplace morale, such as sick-building syndrome, low wages, and employees being mistreated.

The major factors are as under:

I. Job security.

II. Management style.

III. Staff feeling that their contribution is valued by their employer.

IV. Realistic opportunities for merit-based promotion.

V. The perceived social or economic value of the work being done by the organisation as a whole.

VI. The perceived status of the work being done by the organisation as a whole.

VII. Team composition.

VIII. The work culture.

Family Welfare

In case of corporates, the term 'family welfare' translates into a practical term such as medical and insurance facilities for the employees, assisting them in housing and other matters that make them comfortable in mind and body.

Esprit de corps

The kind of esprit de corps found in the army is not easy to inculcate. However, team spirit is essential for great work in companies. Towards this, many companies have a get-together of a team at regular intervals, some training residential workshops, fun evenings, and such activities. The managers can encourage such spirit by getting to know the employees working under them, chatting with employees on subjects other than work-related issues and sharing time during meals.

Leading by example

Leading - and living - by example means your team knows that you'll also do whatever you expect from them to do. Only then will they work hard to help you achieve the mission.

For instance, if you ask a co-worker to do something, make sure you'd be willing to do it yourself. Or if you implement new rules for the office, then follow those rules just as closely as you expect everyone else to follow them.

Look closely at your own behaviour. If you criticize people for interrupting, but you constantly do it yourself, you need to fix this. Yes, you want people to pay attention to one another and listen to all viewpoints, so demonstrate this yourself.

Subordinates interpret everything a leader does in a manner they want. They will modify their own behaviour based upon their individual motivations and assessments. Leaders must project an unshakeable belief that the mission can and will be accomplished. Subordinates will also naturally seek to emulate the behaviour of a successful leader, and try to equal or surpass his/her accomplishments or skills at their respective levels.

The doctrines that we have seen earlier, meant for service officers, can and do work for managers too. Following as many of these guidelines as possible will turn a manager into a leader and foster loyalty.

❐

The Second Level

Change Communication – Lessons from Experience

The focus of Business Communication is to improve business, and when business encounters change, communication aims to make the change process more effective.

Why do change management programs fail?

When change is eminent, planned or otherwise, there is always a conflict between the 'business status quo' and planning for tomorrow while changing today. It is always easier to maintain business as usual. To make changes in the present systems or any other business elements would mean either keeping the ongoing work on hold or making extra time and effort for something that may take some time to show results. This implies time off from immediate returns.

Change involves people. It has to begin at a personal level. After all, the organisations are what the people are. They can easily take the organisation through change smoothly or they can put so many spokes that the management may abandon the change effort altogether. Finally, every individual has to take decision for action. This depends on the agenda that each person has decided for oneself. For this decision, people will want to know if they are to gain or lose as the effect of change. If there is no gain for an individual, there will not be much enthusiasm for change. **'What is in it for me?'** is the driver for action.

Different people have differing views about any proposed change. However, the default attitude is generally of resistance. And the reason is that most of the change programs do not take into account people's opinions or seek their involvement right from the beginning. Nobody welcomes being told to change. That tends to harden the attitude. Diverse outlooks and concerns have effect on individual agendas and outcomes. People move on.

The failure to change efforts is mainly due to the human element. The employees feel that the change is not essential and there is no need to make all the efforts. They are also prone to misunderstand their role in the process of change. They look upon change as something temporary and feel that they can somehow manage to go on till this thing blows over. Frequent change means the responsibilities of employees increase and that is why they resist it. Another important reason is that their opinion was not taken before the process of change was initiated.

Also communication is expensive. It takes up valuable time. Proper communication needs dedicated time. This impinges on time that can be utilised for direct business activities. Though instructional communication takes less time, any other form of communication has opportunity costs.

Explicit information gets communicated very easily. This means instructions, manuals, and methods can be passed on very easily. However, the subtleties of the task, some experience gained and knowledge stored in the brain may not be passed on at all! This may be because it is not easy to put such knowledge into words. To begin with, it needs to be assimilated and understood before it can be properly communicated. Once again this becomes a time-consuming process. Passing on implicit knowledge also encounters another problem. This is the 'everybody knows' syndrome. This means that one does not find it necessary to communicate implicit knowledge in a belief that **'since I know this, others must know it too'**. This may or may not be true. This syndrome is also applicable to explicit communication.

Deciding on a message to communicate in itself is not enough. Now what is required is a vehicle or channel of communication. This vehicle means a platform for communication that has become a part of regular work process. However, having a vehicle for communication and using it are two different things.

People's resistance to change – especially in an organisation during the process of organisational reshuffle – is the manifestation of **'fear of the unknown'**. This fear leads to **'fear of not being in control'. Fear of the unknown may have many causes** – it has its seed in lack of information that may be perceived by different individuals as threats to status or fear of failure or simply as lack of perceived benefits. Another fall-out of this fear of the unknown is that people feel they are no longer in control of the situation and are being used as pawns by outside forces and this induces a deep-rooted resistance and they use their 'will to co-operate' as their ultimate tool – by simply not co-operating!

Here is an example of an advertising company owned by a Marwari. Marwaris are known to be orthodox and follow traditional methods in their business. This company had many restrictions on employees. They had to address their seniors properly, dress conservatively, bring only vegetarian lunch, have tea/coffee breaks at set times and so on. This company was taken over by a multinational group and all these restrictions vanished. The open culture of the multinational group was suddenly thrust upon them. Surprisingly, the employees who earlier complained about the restrictions, now sought them. Even the non-vegetarian employees, who could now bring meat and chicken, continued with their previous practice. This was just resistance to change. Along with this ingrained opposition to change was the fact that the acquisition by the multinational was not explained to the employees. The reasons, the changes and the different management style, nothing was communicated.

The failure of change initiatives is also due to imbalanced communication strategies that stress on aims and visions but leave out the nitty-gritty of how the change is to be accomplished. Clever language and tall claims do not explain the actual steps that need to be taken. This gives rise to cynicism.

Having a well-researched, workable business solution, process or system change plan is not a guarantee for success. The status quo is comfortable for employees as they are familiar with it. Change will make a difference, but whether it will be to their advantage or not is not known. Hence, the resistance! The middle managers have their own rationale for opposing change. They think they might lose their power or that they might face redundancy.Even the executives are not open about their support to the change. They may seem to uphold it initially but soon tend to lose track with day-to-day business compulsions. Added to this is the stress of change program on the available resources and time. The organisation's top management may want to spend more time and resources on the revenue generating activities. It means that the change program that may be the right approach for the company for its tomorrow, gets a backseat today.

Effective communication smoothens change

Communication is the most important ingredient for success of any change plan. It has to be felt in every part of the business. It has to be noticed at every point. It has to be all-encompassing to make any change successful.

Knowledge of what is in store for tomorrow prepares the mind to adjust to the change. It really makes no difference who will benefit from the change and who will not, change is still perceived as a threat in either case. However, there is a solution to lessen this perception, and that is effective communication. The right kind of communication certainly makes it easy for the affected to adapt to change. Whatever the scope of change, communicating about it will take care of the ingrained resistance to change. A complete and extensive change that touches all aspects of the organisation, such as a merger or acquisition, can be made smoother by communicating about it. Even a small change, such as a system change or introduction of some new technology, which may need training but will not be very exhaustive, will be more acceptable if backed by proper communication.

'Continuous improvement' is a change process that requires coming together of knowledge, skills and responsibility across the organisation. These need to work in sync in the process of the development and progress, which is possible only with the right kind of communication. In fact, communication should not stop after initial smoothening change process but should be continued so that the results of change can be gauged through the response generated.

These responses can then be examined and evaluated. The results can determine whether the change is achieving what was expected or if some modifications are necessary.

When the employees feel, rightly or wrongly, vulnerable, they need assurance. A proper communication plan can give this assurance.

If the management does not have enough information about the change, they may wish to desist from communicating anything. That is dangerous not only for the change program but also for the employee morale. Everyone wants to know what is happening, and what is going to happen. If there is no information forthcoming from the top, then the grapevine will have a field day. When the picture is not clear, the employees will fill in any colours they choose.

The most important issue is letting everyone know what is happening. Let them know what is in store, what to expect. If change is eminent, people will need to know how it is going to affect them. Then they can prepare themselves to deal with it. If the management does not have all the answers, that also needs to be told. Let the employees know that you do not have all the answers. It is important to be sensitive to the impact of your announcements on them, especially those employees who would be the most affected by change.

Another extremely important issue is the timing of communicating change. It is best to communicate early in the change process and communicate to all employees at the same time. It is definitely a better proposition to let the employees hear about it from the management rather than a filtered or subverted version from some other source.

In organisations with **'an overall philosophy and strategy to guide communication planning, systems and processes'**, communication is not just giving topical information. It is a well thought out and well planned activity that is meant to ensure that the employees understand the company culture, its philosophy, the nature of its products and services, its customer profile and the business.

The globalisation of corporate environment has increased the importance of corporate communication. The necessity to run the business from different geographical locations means getting work done from culturally different workforce. Technology becomes important to carry out communication, and the corporate focus shifts to employees, who will send and receive communication. Internet and Intranet assume a very important role as the preferred means of communication for voice and data.

Internal communication and change management both are influenced by common factors such as existing business conditions, the culture and structure of the organisation, and the leadership and management styles. Changes resulting from mergers and acquisitions, especially bad ones such as redundancies inevitably bring about negativity and uncertainty. This gives rise to absenteeism; in the process, turnover and productivity suffer. Open and honest communication can help to a great extent.

There is never any chance of too much communication. It is important that the information given is accurate and honest and timely. Communication should be regarded as an ongoing process and not as a one-off event. A properly planned communication will be more beneficial than any newsletters, memos and bulletins by themselves. That is why, it is vital to have a proper communication plan delineating the present state of the organisation and where it is planning to go and by what means.

Audience concerns are very important

Any communication process is more effective when designed specifically for the target audience. This is more so when an organisational change is imminent. The instinctive employee reaction is: *"What is in it for me?"* From the employee's point of view, any change is a risk. This perceived risk is viewed as a threat. The severity of this threat perception is considerably reduced if there is a benefit attached to it. It is even more important that the benefit accrues to those who have to undertake the change. If it is seen that while they are facing the change, some others are reaping the fruits of their labour, then the fairness factor comes into play and the original negativity is increased manifold.

Geographical and cultural diversities need different treatment to be given to communication. Each culture and language may not receive a merely translated message in a similar manner. In fact, that kind of translation done without paying any attention to the cultural differences and the language tenor may have unexpected results, not always desirable.

Manyatimes, the employee responses to change announcements seem absolutely unwarranted to the management. The reactions are not what the management expects or even foresees. There does not seem to be any rational explanation to the disproportionate reaction. This, however, is easily explained. When people face a threatening situation or perceive themselves at a great danger and feel themselves not in control, they experience what is termed as 'mental noise'. This noise creates disturbance in the process of assimilating information and only 80% of information is understood. The remaining 20% also is not focused on the issues that the management feels are relevant, but is focused on more personal and immediate concerns.

Who informs about change is very important

One of the most important aspects of change communication is the source. Who imparts the information is vital. Most employees prefer their direct supervisor to inform them of any company news and programs. Case studies, surveys and research prove that while going through a transformation, the best person to communicate this is the direct boss.

Three serious mistakes that can harm the change communication process:

Many CEOs advised by the senior HR professionals take the extreme step of directly communicating with the employees. This is an error that creates two problems. The employee may look on this as merely an empty gesture, a placating strategy. However, the worst impact will be on the employee-supervisor relationship. As workers want to work for someone, who is connected and has a degree of power within the organisation, direct communication from HR personnel might indicate that their supervisor does not have much importance in the organisation.

The second mistake is that sometimes the senior management may advocate equality and will have the employees and supervisors sitting together to hear the news. This undoubtedly undermines the supervisor's authority and consequently, their influence on the employees reduces. This clearly does not help during the actual change process because the employees feel that they know as much as their supervisor.

The third mistake is the information overload through indirect media: brochures, reports, bulletins, videos, guidebooks and team briefing outlines. This kind of overzealous approach too is not the right way. The bewildered employee is not amused. There is too much information. A face-to-face communication with the supervisor is critical.

Effective communication is not the responsibility solely of the communications department. This department in the traditional organisations is generally quite apart from the other departments. It probably does not interact on a regular basis with the employees. It lacks trust and connections across the organisation for such an important task.

Day-to-day communication can follow the hierarchical steps from top to bottom, from the top management to the employees via the middle management and supervisors. However, for a major change, the middle manager step should be bypassed and the communication should go directly from the top management to the supervisors. This will avoid any filtering, and unintended or otherwise modification of the message. The supervisors necessarily have to be apprised before the employees so that their authority remains unaltered. Employees are definitely interested in knowing about change relative to their area of work.

The most reliable source of communication for an employee is their immediate superior. If these frontline managers and supervisors are not convinced about the need or benefits of the intended change, then nothing will make the employee feel positive about it.

Face-to-face communication is important

Face-to-face communication always scores over any other type of communication. This is especially true when uncertainty rules and the employees are in a suspicious state of mind. At such times, a medium of communication other than face-to-face may filter or distort the intended message.

Communication as a process is innately complicated. There are many layers of filters that interfere with the process. These are 'attitudes, preconceived notions, mood, background noise, interruptions'. When a large number of employees are involved and the interference is compounded by their fears, anxieties, tiredness, and/or disinterest, then the process increases in complexity. Only a small percentage (7%) of any message is conveyed by the actual words used. The rest of the interpretation depends upon the way the words are uttered and the non-verbal body language. So, a written message loses out on the important aspects of communication interpretation and this may lead to the receivers drawing their own meaning from the message.

The communication programs should revolve around direct and personal face-to-face communication, simply because such communication carries weight and is more convincing than any other type of communication. This is more important during the early stages of any change communication where establishing trust is more important. This also allows for a dialogue and clearing of any doubts.

An information dispensing process does not qualify as communication. Right information, nicely and effectively worded, does not mean that communication has been effected. This is so especially in times of change when stress levels are quite high. The IT capability may have refined and speeded up, but the human brain cannot keep up with the speed. We still remain in the Stone Age when it comes to threat perception and the methods of dealing with it.

What does this imply? That our speed of understanding and processing information has not kept pace with the speed of communication or the efficiency of IT. In fact, during times of stress, the speed of assimilating information goes further down. At such times, increasing the efficiency of communication is certainly not the answer. What will make a difference is some low-tech face-to-face communication. This kind of personal dialogue is essential to overcome the 'mental noise' that clouds the judgement of the employees and filters the information received. The mental noise also can twist and give an unwanted connotation to the message. To combat all these problems of miscommunication and communication barriers that threaten the message, face-to-face communication is the best remedy. That is the only communication that can convey empathy and care to the employees, the only way where they can voice their concerns and hope to be heard. This makes them perceive that they matter to the management. This establishes trust. The hi-tech IT-based communication methods can only be one-way and impersonal.

Face-to-face communication has to be the foundation on which all other communication activities must be built.

Everybody should be involved

Involvement across the organisation is a forward factor for change management. This is where good communication comes into play. This involvement is not just to implement change but also to formulate change strategy. When this happens, the employees feel responsible to see that the changes are successfully implemented as they have helped in formulating them. Employees across the board should be engaged in the change process right from the strategic decision-making. Maximum number of people should be involved so that more ideas are generated. A bottom to top approach is good.

Staff consultation should occur before any kind of change process is set into motion. This consultation should not be just for the sake of show or pretence. Genuine efforts to get employees involved from the initial stages ensure that the organisation does not lose out on some of the best ideas that the front line employees may have. They do the actual work and may have a better understanding of processes that may work and those that may not.

Some techniques for getting the staff involved include awareness workshops (building on the senior management programs), departmental 'away-days' (where the whole department jointly may stay away from work and do something other than regular work, like discussions, relaxing or even going on picnics), face-to-face interviews and structured staff surveys. The surveys need to be carried out only after a briefing to the employees where they have a chance to ask and argue their point of view. This will help in building a shared agenda for change. Co-opting team members into working groups will ensure staff involvement through to the completion of the agenda.

It is advisable to actively interact with people at all levels in the organisation and seek out their concerns, questions and issues. It is essential that they feel comfortable and safe while voicing their concerns. This may entail getting an outside consultant to take charge of this issue. Confidentiality promises have to be honoured at any cost.

When there is some control over the risk, the perceived threat is lesser than when the risk is involuntary. So, certain knowledge about impeding change can reduce threat perception.

A manager's role in communication is crucial

A manager plays a very significant role during change. The most helpful act by a manager is simply listening to the employees. This makes the employees feel that their concerns are important and are heard by the management. The managers are seen as caring and understanding only by the simple act of listening. Of course, this again reiterates the point that face-to-face communication is better, as IT-based communication cannot generate the same feeling of trust in the employee.

One approach for the managers to communicate with the employees is based on 'four Ps':

The *purpose*: Why do we have to do this?

The *picture*: What will it look and feel like when we reach our goal?

The *plan*: Step-by-step, how we will get there?

The *part*: What can you (and need to) do to help us move forward?

The corporate culture should be favourable to communication at all times and not just restricted to meetings and memos. It should be an intrinsic part of the corporate culture. What matters is connecting with others, and not whether it is good communication or bad.

There is another important communication tenet: Fast and quick communication is certainly advisable but not premature communication. The management has to be completely sure of the facts before they are given out. Uncertainty or vagueness in the message can increase suspicion and anxiety. Premature information may set off a panic wave amongst the employees.

An outside communication consultant is a good idea

An external communications consultant is a good strategy to lead the employees through the process of change. Actively pursuing employees to find out about their problems and their doubts and questions is required. During change, the employees may not feel comfortable voicing their concerns to their managers. An outside consultant is taken as a safe recipient of many problems and issues.

Communication channels are significant

Tony Proctor and *Ioanna Doukakis* researched the introduction of change in a large public sector organisation. The authors found that the traditional cascading down of information about the impeding change was totally inadequate when a companywide reorganisation was involved. The modern communication channels, such as e-mails and Intranet were more effective and management training filled up rest of the void in understanding.

In the earlier process of communication, the message was all-important. The channel of message delivery more often than not was the written word on paper. The time dimension was involved in forming and writing the message and also in the delivery. It took time to write and some more to deliver. Today, it is all about speed. While the core of the message is still very crucial, fast and instant dispersal of messages has become important to conduct business. Global practices, multinational clientele, and accelerating technology have fuelled the need for speed. Technology has offered many channels of communication and dialogue. The choice of the medium depends upon many factors, internal and external. It is vital to make the right choice.

In 1987, *Frank Carrubba* became the Director of the Hewlett-Packard Laboratory, which conducts all the centralised research and development for this key player in the global electronics industries. He conducted a study to understand why some research teams excelled in their performance while other teams with equal measure of talent, experience and expertise performed poorly. The findings confirmed that teams with personal communication amongst themselves and with the client performed beyond their goals. The reason could be that they concentrated on the task at a personal level and had no need to prove anything to anyone.

❐

Essentials of Change Communication

Real-time research in companies that have managed change successfully, came up with many interesting observations. Most of them have a definite communication strategy. Apart from this, there were many common practices that were followed by these companies. Companies were chosen based on their performance in a time interval of five years. The criteria were substantial growth in the last five years in terms of:

(a) Revenue and Profits.

(b) Customer base.

(c) International reach.

(d) Technologies used.

(e) Employee strength.

Communication strategy of each successful company was studied. This was because it has been established that effective communication is essential ingredient for successful change. So, the focus was on:

- What was the expected outcome?
- Was there any planned communication exercise?

- Who initiated communication?
- Which drivers directed the content?
- What was the level of managerial commitment to communication?
- Which were the channels of communication?
- Which channels have maximum impact on the changed behaviour?
- Which factors contributed to the changed behaviour?

The aim of the research was to study the communication channels and the integrated multi-faceted interventions and to assess how these combined information, instruction, collaboration, business process design, feedback and incentive systems helped to facilitate the process of change.

One of the criteria to conduct study in a specific company was the response to contact initiated from the Company website. All these companies responded to online e-mails requesting information and interviews of key personnel. This fact in itself proved that communication was smooth, open and people were easy to access.

The aim was to find out how proper communication impacts successful change. Information about management considerations and choices concerning communication could, thus, be combined with employee preferences to provide a basis for general guidelines on the process of communication.

The purpose of Change Communication

The purpose of Change Communication is to establish timely communication across the organisation and to prepare the employees with skill sets to respond to changes in real time. These simple goals cover a myriad of communication processes that include top to down, down to top and lateral communication.

Each individual company had its own set of communication principles. Varying communication initiatives and channels identified for each company satisfy individual communication preferences.

Common Characteristics

These successful companies have certain common characteristics.

1. A sense of pride in the organisation. Organisational values are instilled in each employee, each new recruit.
2. Access to e-mails. This means direct e-mails to top echelon and a definite response in reasonable timeframe is also available.
3. Training and knowledge sharing.
4. An opportunity for bonding with others is offered very regularly. This includes monthly/quarterly meetings as well as an annual function, which serves multiple purposes.

Common communication practices amongst these companies

1. Top Management Commitment - Clear Goals and Objectives.
2. The Right Content.
3. Open Communication.
4. Multiple Points of Contact.

5. Multiple Channels of Communication.
6. Training.
7. Knowledge Management.
8. Culture-oriented Communication.
9. Involvement.
10. Corporate Communication Department.
11. An Outsider's Perspective.
12. Employee Satisfaction Survey.
13. Employees as Brand Ambassadors.

Top Management Commitment – Clear Goals and Objectives

The top management is committed to communication and is seen and heard to be enthusiastic about the envisioned change. The concerned people believe in the change and are themselves aware of their role during the transformation. Why and how questions about the change have definite answers and exactly what is expected in terms of everyday work profiles is quite clear. As there is no ambiguity at the top, the faith and trust in the change program percolates down.

For example, in case of Zensar, a workforce subjected to change rhetoric once too often was sceptical of the new change propagated by the new CEO, Ganesh Natarajan. Even the top managers had a 'So, what's new?' attitude. Ganesh went about convincing the organisation by starting from top and cascading down detailed information about his plan of changing the basic business model from technology-based to practice-based. This changed the focus from technology to customers. To commence the communication process, Ganesh formed a 'Vision Community', which drew employees from the upper half of the organisation. (Zensar has eight levels of seniority. To begin with, the top four levels contributed to make up the Vision Community and later the employees from the lower four levels too were included.)

The Vision Community designed a detailed presentation telling about why Zensar was doing the change, how it would be organised, what kind of training was involved and what was in it for the employees. The information about who needs to perform what actions during implementation also was included. This clarified the business issues involved and also explained the nitty-gritty of the operation.

In the case of Tata Consultancy Services, the top executives made a Transition Road Map. This necessarily meant that they had to be absolutely clear about the process of the envisioned change. Without this awareness, it would not have been possible to draw out the future map and explain the means of achieving the stated vision. The message that they wanted to convey was that, without change, there is no survival.

The Right Content

The focus was seen to be on communicating the right content. Just high business issues and business model descriptions do not move the employees. They need to know the reasons simply because they are educated and qualified technologists, who may not accept anything blindfolded. They need to know the why, how, what, where, who, and 'what's in it for me?' of any change initiative. What made the difference were the answers to: What is in it for me? What exactly is my work profile?

Communication and coordination practices were institutionalised to ensure that they are performed as managed processes. The content communicates the values of the organisation. All the companies showcase the organisational values. The values are included in the orientation training as well as management training. This generates an awareness of the guiding principles for work.

A noticeable communication property was that the content was not just 'FYI' (for your information) but conveyed the expected behaviour as well as instructed on the work requirements.

Open Communication

An important aspect of these organisations that have experienced success in their change initiatives is the stress on 'open communication' and 'direct access' to top management. The e-mails are read and seen. All these companies have excellent communication process in place. All change savvy companies have sophisticated top-down and bottom-up strategies for communication.

The employees are aware of this direct access facility and are certain of a response. This ensures open communication and a sense of comfort for an employee. The most junior employee too has the right to be heard and has no fear of reprisal. The communication can remain confidential if so desired by the individual. So, individuals or groups are able to raise concerns and have them addressed by management.

Apart from this upward communication, the employees have the benefit of the Intranet, where technical and personal communications are allowed. A feeling of being heard is important. Employees tend to share jokes, experiences and seek technical solutions too on the Intranet.

However, one important aspect is the 'need to know' communication despite the label of open communication.

As Dr. F.C. Kohli put it, *"The employee need not know I am going to take over some company tomorrow. That is beyond his pale of necessary information."*

Multiple Points of Contact

Face-to-face and individual communication at many points seems to be a common thread running through these organisations. Annual get-togethers, weekly/bi-monthly/quarterly meetings, games, coming together for cultural activities, and other communication avenues generate a feeling of belonging. These work-related as well as social exchanges not only smoothen the work related activities but also develop a social relationship and human bonding, which is conducive to work. At Tata Consultancy Services (TCS), 'people engagement program' and, at least, one specific organised event a month constitute the informal communication that leads to bonding.

Forward-looking companies promote a strong culture of internal cooperation between employees and business units, and external cooperation with industry consortia and universities. Formal contact comprises the CEO e-mails about some companywide issues, e-mails from executive management about policy decisions, news updates, the happenings in the company that are of general interest, work related instructions from project heads and customer queries. However, restricting contact only to formal communication is not the norm in successful companies.

With the increasing size of a company, the formal and organised nature of regular contact certainly goes on increasing. Spontaneous meetings between top management necessarily have to make way for a scheduled address by the CEO. The supervisors and the Group-heads then have to look after the day-to-day work communication.

Multiple Channels of Communication

The companies that have successfully carried out change initiatives are seen to utilise multiple channels of communication. The message is repeated and completely drilled into the psyche of the employee. While CEO mails, news bulletins, pinup notices and such media give the general information about the change, e-mails from supervisors and even the Intranet elaborate on how the work is to be carried out vis-à-vis the change. Change is, thus, integrated at work level and is not restricted at enterprise level. Without this clear aim, any change would have remained just rhetoric!

It is a good idea to utilise the internal portal for change communication. The questions regarding the change can be anticipated and answered. This reassures the employees.

Training

As the company grows, training gets more and more formal. The size of the organisation commands the kind and the method of training. Smaller companies can afford to have on-the-job training, whereas bigger companies need group training at designated company infrastructure. Multinational massive companies have a great number of trainees. The vast geographical spread and the sheer number of trainees may necessitate a separate training facility. It is advisable to have a mentor for each trainee. This relationship should be carried further till the need for it is felt.

The common practice amongst these companies is that the initial training consists of technical training as well as life skills or soft skills training. The latter includes managerial skills training amongst others. Nowadays the training includes understanding of other cultures. The further training is generally need-based. When a new project comes, the skills required should be reviewed and a 'gap analysis' carried out. Depending on that, training should be designed.

Knowledge Management

In any present-day organisation, knowledge repository is an important asset. Knowledge databases should be maintained either on the internal server or in a dedicated library. If the need arises, any employee should be able to refer to necessary information. The amount of information is not as important as the structure of the information available. What is more relevant is how to find, analyse, decipher and transform the information into actions required to carry out the work in hand.

Companies need to have robust connectivity for the employees to the Intranet and to standardise knowledge repositories, and communities of practice. Substantial time and equipment investments need to be made in the KM systems. Companies need to evolve sophisticated strategies to manage content. These include technical knowledge repositories, knowledge base for technical support, and Project Closure Documents (PCD). Knowledge support to assist busy employees in creating, editing and translating knowledge assets will also go a long way.

Culture-oriented Communication

The employee profile of many organisations has become global in composition over the last few years. This has necessitated communication with a certain awareness of the cultural differences. This is more important for teams working with members separated geographically and culturally. For example, a Japanese and an Indian working on the same project will need to have a common language and an understanding of each other's culture. Many times, an Indian employee may have to deal with antagonism from the client or team member for some imagined wrongs.

Sometimes, even with common language, social issues and culture can lead to amusing faux pas. For example, in one company, when one project was successfully completed, an e-mail from the MD describing the success in cricketing terms just did not go down well with the American counterparts. There was complete non-comprehension.

The organisations generally deal with this problem by giving cultural inputs during the initial training. The culture-oriented training can also be need-based.

Involvement

A culture of knowledge-centricity and innovation right from the top levels of the management was present in all these companies. Each and every employee had to be involved in the transformation. This means communication had to reach the last employee. Zensar took care of this when the Company launched its change program. The 'Vision Community' made set presentation to all the employees in batches and fielded questions till everyone was satisfied.

The multiple geographical locations of TCS and the sheer number of employees compelled the Company to evolve some effective method to reach everyone. The Corporate Communications department invited volunteers from amongst the employees globally to act as a link between the Company and the grass root employees. 42 of those who applied were selected, trained in communication and appointed as 'Communication Coordinators'.

Corporate Communication Department

In case of TCS, it was decided to bring in an outsider to steer the change. The process began with the formation of 'Corporate Communications' department. This was completely separate from the HR department, though both the departments worked in close coordination to ensure that the change communication was relevant and reached the 'last mile'. Corporate Communications played a crucial role in successful change management. The content, the method, the media, the timings of communiqués - all were decided by the Corporate Communications along with the VP Transformation.

Similarly, in Zensar, the Corporate Communication was delinked from the Human Resources department to exploit its potential fully and was made more employee-oriented. The entire Change Management Communication was conceptualised here with close coordination of the 'Vision Community'.

Similarly, at another company, Corporate Communications department was involved in conducting an 'Employee Satisfaction Survey' and designing the communication initiatives based on the findings.

An Outsider's Perspective

People don't resist change; they resist being changed in the process. Since it is difficult to get an insider to objectively carry out the process of challenging existing habits, TCS roped in an outsider to bring a fresh perspective to the change program. The role of this person was to act as a facilitator and a change agent.

Persistent Systems Private Limited (PSPL) brought in an outside consultant, as it did not have a separate Corporate Communications Department. This allowed its people to pursue project related technical activity. Most important was the fact that the company needed an outsider's perspective, as its ethos was still of a small company.

Employee Satisfaction Survey

'Employee Satisfaction Survey' helped the companies modify and, in some cases, initiate communication. Zensar realised the 'Level 3' employees' discontent and took steps to rectify the matter by scheduling meetings with this group and discussing the issue. This gave rise to a group 'Power of Three' which communicated with each other and with the top management via a password protected access on the Company Intranet. The dissatisfaction levels dropped and the power of these managers was utilised towards better fulfilment of the project demands. Technical discussions and helping each other with definite solutions was achieved.

At i-flex, this survey brought out the need of the employees for more group-wise communication. This gave rise to scheduled group-wise meetings conducted by the Group head.

At TCS, many issues crop up during 'Employee Satisfaction Survey'. Appropriate steps are taken. However, the matter does not rest here. These remedial measures are informed through the monthly reports that are distributed across the company. This kind of update is important and it makes the employee certain that his/her grievances are given due attention.

Employees as Brand Ambassadors

This is the most interesting communication application with great impact. The employees of an organisation are undoubtedly the best brand ambassadors of the Company. At i-flex and TCS, the awareness of this fact is very high. These companies ensure that the internal brand awareness is given high priority. Constant updates on the company's brand, its achievements, progress and changes initiated are communicated to all the employees on a regular basis. Any employee can interact anytime with an outsider (including customers) backed by a thorough knowledge of the Company.

One more important aspect is that a feeling of pride and belonging is carefully nurtured in employees. This is done via impromptu meetings; chat sessions, discussion forums, where the top management and employees have a healthy give and take and also fun sessions where bonding is increased. The vision and values of the organisation are conveyed all the time and act as behavioural guiding principles.

Employee Point of View

Informal discussions with the employees of Zensar, PSPL, TCS and Cirrus Logic have thrown up some interesting facts about communication.

- There is open communication amongst the juniormost employees. As they rise in hierarchy, the openness diminishes. A healthy acceptance of needing help or input from others, which is present amongst employees, becomes a matter of prestige. *"How can I ask for help? What will others think of me?"* prevents the line managers or team leaders from seeking help.
- The entry-level employees do not see any problem in communication, but as they become older in the organisation, they feel that communication needs to be more open.
- Surprisingly, the print magazine is more popular than e-mails giving the same news.

- Strategic information and media are not as important as information that clearly states the expected action. 'Why are we changing?' is important but employees preferred content that was specific, easy-to-understand, consistent, clear and timely.
- Employees are comfortable with interactions that are open, candid, two-way and face-to-face.
- Junior level employees do not read all the corporate e-mails and electronic newsletters. They read e-mails only if it concerns their immediate interests and projects.
- Many junior employees were not overtly concerned with CMM certification or any management initiatives. They were just interested in knowing about their projects and their skill sets.
- Junior employees do not always attend all-company open forums. Group Open forums are better attended and team meetings, even informal ones, are always attended.
- While there were exceptions, overwhelmingly the participants described communications that increased complexity as message and media-driven. Again and again, they told us this message-based approach has very little impact on the work decisions they make or on their performance. The workforce is seeking communication that they can use to get stuff done.

❐

The Third Level: Work Communication

The day-to-day communication or the work communication needs to follow the principles of effective communication. Apart from following the C-commandments of Completeness, Correctness, Conciseness, Consideration, Concreteness, Clarity, and Courteousness, work communication needs to follow 'Basic Communication Guidelines':

- Use short sentences. More than fifteen words in a sentence reduce the clarity of the meaning. After drafting your communication, seek out commas and 'ands', and replace with full stops.

- Write as you would speak – but ensure it is grammatically correct. Don't try to be formal. Don't use old-fashioned figures of speech. We no longer refer to ourselves as 'the undersigned', nor do we use words such as 'aforementioned', or 'your goodselves'. We do not sign off with 'I remain yours sincerely' and similar phrases. You should show that you're living in the same century as the reader.

- As to how informal to be, for example, writing much like normal every day speech (for example, don't, let's, I'd, we've), bear in mind that some older people, and younger people, who have inherited traditional views, could react less favourably to a writing style, which they consider to be the product of laziness or poor education. Above all, it is important to write in a style that the reader is likely to find agreeable.

- Avoid jargons, acronyms, technical terms unless absolutely essential.
- DO NOT USE ALLCAPS – even for headings. Words formed of capital letters are difficult to read because there are no word-shapes, just blocks of text. (We read quickly by seeing word shapes, not the individual letters.)
- Sans serif fonts (like Arial, Helvetica and Tahoma) are modern, and will give a modern image. Serif fonts (like Garamond, Goudy and Times) are older, and will tend to give a less modern image.
- Sans serif fonts take longer to read, so being modern may extract a price. This is because we have all grown up learning to read serif fonts. Serif fonts also have a horizontal flow, which helps readability and reading comfort. (Serif fonts developed before the days of print, when the engraver needed to create a neat exit from each letter.)
- Avoid fancy fonts. They may look clever or innovative, but they are more difficult to read, and some are nearly impossible.
- Use 10-12 point size for body copy (text). 14-20 point is fine for the main headings, bold or normal. Sub-headings should be in 10-12 bold type.
- Any printed material looks very untidy if you use more than two different fonts and two different point sizes. Generally, the fewer the better!

- If your organisation stipulates a 'house' font, then use it. If your organisation doesn't, then it should!
- Black text on a white background is the easiest colour combination to read. Definitely avoid coloured backgrounds.
- Avoid background graphics or pictures behind the text.
- Italics are less easy to read. So is heavy bold type.
- If you must break any of these font rules, do so only for the heading.
- Limit main attention-grabbing headings to no more than fifteen words.
- In letters, position your main heading between two-thirds and three-quarters up the page. This is where the eye is naturally drawn first.
- Use left-justified text, as this is the easiest to read.
- Avoid fully justified text as it creates uneven word spaces and is more difficult to read.
- Remember that effectively written communication enables the reader to understand your meaning in as few words as possible.

❐

E-mails

E-mail has emerged as the most convenient communication tool in business and in social communication. E-mails are fast and easy. They can also be fuming and furious! The very speed can rapidly spread confusion and chaos, gossip and rumours. There is no 'undo' as yet. (Google engineers are working on some such quick recall.)

Unintentional use of 'Reply All' can ruin your career or your reputation. Angry, hurried, unthinking responses – known as flaming – can lead to friends and colleagues turning away from you. There is no recall and damage control can become awkward. Or important e-mail may get dumped as spam because you either left your subject line blank or wrote it without considering the implications.

How do you avoid all such consequences? How do you ensure that your mail is read and appreciated? Many users still pay little attention to proper e-mail technique and correct e-mail etiquette. There are certain norms to be followed and certain rules to be observed while writing e-mails and responding to them.

Important points to remember are:

- People get too many e-mails.
- The attention span of the receiver for an e-mail is quite short.
- Once you hit 'send', there is no second chance.

The essentials of effective communication that we have studied, of course, hold true for e-mails too. Each e-mail should be correct, complete, concrete, clear, concise (very crucial), courteous and considerate. However, the very nature of the medium makes some changes essential. The ease and informality of e-mails is not necessarily a license to use casual language and untidy format. Standards of professionalism for business e-mails and common decency for social e-mails should be scrupulously maintained.

Some guidelines to follow

Subject line

This is the most important line, which tells the receiver what the e-mail is about. In these days of increased spam and unsolicited mails, it is crucial that your mail is not sent to the bin. A meaningful subject line would ensure that your mail is read. A few well-chosen words can tell the receiver at once about the content. If you make appropriate use of the subject line, you increase the chances that your e-mail will be read, rather than mistaken for spam and deleted without so much as a glance.

People, who get a lot of e-mails, scan the subjectline in order to decide whether to open, forward, file, or trash a message. If your subject line is vague – or even worse, if it's blank – you have missed your first opportunity to inform or persuade your reader. Remember – your message is not the only one in your recipient's mailbox. Hence, before you hit 'send', ensure a subject line that accurately describes the content.

Absolute no-nos

Blank subject line

Example 1: Absolutely avoid. Might go directly to spam.

From	Hema Hirlekar (hemahirlekar@pmail.com)
To	shirinjoshi@pmail.com
cc	
Bcc	
Subject	

The recipient's spam detector might consign it to spam immediately. If it doesn't, then the receiver will trash it.

Example 2: Still not appropriate for business e-mail.

Subject	Important, read immediately

Vague subject line is not really effective: 'Hi', 'Hello', 'FYI', 'Important, read immediately', 'Just one question', 'Follow-up', 'Update'. Again, if it is a close friend, family, then hi, hello is fine.

Example 3: Confusing.

Subject	Just one question/Update

'Just one question' – about what? 'Follow-up, update' – on what?

Also avoid using URGENT and IMPORTANT. Even more so than the high-priority option, you must, at all times, try to avoid these types of words in an e-mail or subject line unless it is a really, really urgent or important message.

Meaningful subject line

Example 1: This e-mail is a response to a query from a prospective customer, by ABC Company. There is no likelihood that such an e-mail would be ignored.

Subject	Answer to your query on schemes from ABC Company for broadband.

Example 2: This is an internal mail in a company. What does EOM mean? It means 'End of Message'. That means the recipient need not even open the mail as all the information is in the subject line.

Subject	Meeting on project X on 13th Jan. in Conference hall at 10 AM – EOM

Example 3: If your message is one of a regular series of e-mails, such as a weekly project report, include the date in the subject line.

Subject	Project CRM update – 20th Jan., 2012

Example 4: For a message that needs a response, you might want to include a call to action.

Subject	Project XYZ update – Please reply by 15th Mar., 2012

Content

As the attention span for an e-mail is quite short, it is essential that the very first paragraph contains the essence of the message. If this has spiked the receiver's interest, they will read further. The skill lies in wording this paragraph with utmost care. It is almost like writing a précis of the précis.

Example 1:

The sales meeting on 13th Jan. highlighted the need for more sales representatives in the Western region. The ad for new sales jobs will be placed on *www.jobs.com* from 10th Jan. for five consecutive days. Newspaper ads will be placed in the second phase from 20th Feb.

After this first paragraph, the mail goes on to describe other details, such as the job requirements, ad agency, etc. This was an FYI e-mail. Different types of e-mails need different details in the first paragraph. Here are some helpful hints for a good start:

- To respond to a letter of complaint:
  Thank you for writing to us about your experience with our service centre at M.G. Road on 23rd Dec.
- To say thank you:
  Thank you so much for donating for our 'save girl child' campaign.
- To confirm an agreement:
  Thank you for your recent tender application with our organisation. I am pleased to confirm that your agency, ABC Ltd. has been appointed as the sole provider of broadband services to us for 1 year, starting today.
- To share information:
  I received some important information regarding outpatients male/female ratio from Dr. Sathe, and I believe it will be useful to you as you analyse the outpatient data.
- To explain a change in policy:

XYZ Bank values your patronage. Hence, we wish to inform you about the change in the Credit Card policy.

- To request:
  I have written a book on classical music. I shall be grateful if you would write a 'Foreword' for it.

- To deny a request:
  Thank you for your invitation to attend the workshop on 'Active listening.' Due to prior engagement, I am unable to attend.

- To respond to a job advertisement:
  I fully meet or exceed the requirements of the Business Analyst III position, and I wish to apply for it.

- To apologise:
  Please accept my apologies for missing the meeting yesterday. I am very sorry that I was unable to attend.

- To congratulate:
  Congratulations on successfully passing your bar exam. You are now officially an attorney!

The first sentences many a times seem challenging and may confound you. The way out is to write the remaining e-mail and then get back to the beginning. Now, it will be easy to form the first sentence.

If you have an important message and expect a response, then it is better to have just that one point in the e-mail. This makes it easy for the recipient to respond. Otherwise, she may hit the reply button at the first point that needs response.

Bad Example:

<table>
<tr><td>Subject</td><td>Comments on your manuscript – Communication</td></tr>
<tr><td colspan="2">Hi Hema,

Thanks for sending the manuscript titled, 'Communication'. I read through it yesterday and feel that you need to be more interesting in the 'Introduction'. The tone could be less text-bookish and more affable. Could you rewrite this chapter and send?

Also, I wanted to let you know that I've scheduled a meeting with the publicity department for this Friday, regarding the marketing campaign for your book. It's at 11:00, and will be in my office.

Please let me know if you can make that time.

Best regards,

Sudheer</td></tr>
</table>

When I receive such an e-mail, I immediately go to my manuscript and begin going through the chapter that needs rewriting. The second part of the e-mail gets overlooked and, hence, remains unanswered. A better method would be to change the first paragraph and mention both the issues. Then use bullets or numbered list. This makes each point stand out, significantly increasing the likelihood that each point will be addressed. Otherwise, one e-mail per point is an option.

Subject	Need answer for two points – manuscript changes and meeting with the publicist
Hi Hema, Thanks for sending the manuscript titled, 'Communication'. I read through it yesterday and feel that you need to be more interesting in the 'Introduction'. The tone could be less text-bookish and more affable. Could you rewrite this chapter and send? Also, I wanted to let you know that I've scheduled a meeting with the publicist for this Friday, regarding marketing campaign for your book. It's at 11:00, and will be my office. Please let me know if you can make that time. Best regards, Sudheer	

Incomplete information in an e-mail will result in many to and fro e-mails. Here is an example:

From	joshi123@pmail.com
Subject Proposal	
Hi, Did you get our proposal for interior decoration last week? If you are interested, can you call me so that we can discuss further? Thanks, Sudheer	

Above is a classic example of an e-mail that may go unanswered. Or else the recipient may ask for clarifications.

More appropriate would be to write the company name in 'From' and a specific 'Subject'.

<table>
<tr><td>From</td><td>Sudheer Joshi from Rhythm Interiors (joshi123@pmail.com)</td></tr>
<tr><td>Subject</td><td>Our proposal for interior decoration of your office at 34, Pawan Street, Pune - 411000 sent on 12th Dec., 2011</td></tr>
<tr><td colspan="2">Dear Mr. Hirlekar

This is with reference to our proposal sent in response to your RFP in the Times on 5th Dec. We have sent our proposal on 12th Dec. We hope you have received it. We have not heard back and wanted to check if you have indeed received our proposal.

If it is convenient, could you call us on the numbers given below? Or let us know a suitable time to call, so that we can call you to discuss further.

Thanks and regards,
Sudheer Joshi
Partner, Rhythm Interiors
123, Sawan Street,
Pune - 411000
Contact:
Landline: 12345678
Cell: 9876543210
Fax: 23456789</td></tr>
</table>

Language

As we have seen in the communication essentials, the language should be correct in grammar, tone, facts and numbers. Just because the medium seems informal, the language need not be thus.

Avoid using short forms and SMS language in an official e-mail. Use standard capitalisation and spelling. Don't say, *"Gr8 spkin 2 u. thx 4 ur help."* This kind of e-mail will put off the recipient.

Attachments

- Attachments should be generally avoided unless absolutely necessary. Some companies have a firewall that quarantines messages with attachment.
- Instead of attaching a file that your reader will have to download and open in a separate program, it is a good idea to just copy-paste the most important part of the document into the body of your message.
- If the attachment is absolutely imperative, then attaching it is fine. You could even send an e-mail to apprise the receiver that you will send an attachment if the receiver would accept.
- Regarding attachments, one has to remember that now many people read e-mails on their mobile phones/ portable devices. They will open the attachment only if they actually need to view the full file for a reason. Do not attach a file just because it is convenient for you to do so.
- Check the size of the attachment if it needs to be sent and compress it by using zip or rar program. For photos, it is easy to reduce the pixel size before sending.
- Attach files in a format only if you know the other side has the software to view! For example, not everyone has MS Publisher, Excel or PowerPoint. If the other side does not have these programs, they most likely cannot open it. Use PDF when possible.

- Be sure your virus, adware and spyware programs are up-to-date and include scanning of your e-mails and attachments, both incoming and outgoing.
- It is better to spread multiple attachments over several e-mails rather than attaching them all to one e-mail to avoid clogging the pipeline.
- If you do need to send extremely large files, there are a few websites that offer this facility. Then, you can just inform the receiver to download it from the site. (One useful site is www.YouSendIt.com)

Signature

Signature files can be attached to every outgoing message, containing contact details and other relevant information. If you are in business, you should almost certainly use an e-mail signature in your communications. It is a great way to draw attention to products or services you offer, and you are making yourself easier to contact as well.

Disclaimers

E-mail disclaimers are statements that are either prepended or appended to e-mails. These statements are usually of a legal character but can also be used for marketing purposes.

An e-mail disclaimer is a disclaimer, notice or warning added to an outgoing e-mail to form a distinct section separate from the main message. The reasons for adding such a disclaimer include confidentiality, copyright, contract formation, defamation, discrimination, harassment, privilege and viruses. Since the disclaimer is usually attached at the end, it will not be noticed until after everything else, the legalese can neither prevent any virus infection or other damage nor restore confidentiality.

However, disclaimers may not be legally enforceable.

For more information, visit: www.e-maildisclaimers.com

Some protocols to observe

- Make sure your e-mail includes a simple, courteous greeting and closing. Helps to make your e-mail not seem demanding or terse. Just add a Hello, (name) or Hi, (name) and your e-mail takes on a completely different tone. It is possible in e-mails to come off as blunt, terse or demanding. Even with everyday e-mails, it is important to make sure that you present yourself with clarity and courtesy.
- Address your contact with the appropriate level of formality and make sure you spell the name correctly.
- Check for the 7 Cs of effective communication. Is your mail Complete, Correct, Concise, Considerate, Concrete, Clear and Courteous?
- Respond immediately. If you have no time or need to check something before replying, still do acknowledge the e-mail saying that you will answer as soon as possible.
- The careless clicking of 'Reply All' option in an e-mail response can create tricky situations. Misunderstandings, inadvertent gossip-mongering may result. Just be cautious.
- However, 'Reply All' is important for many e-mail strings when everybody in the chain needs to know about the developments and progress of that particular subject.
- Do not leave the message thread. Should you include the original message in your reply? Not necessary, if you are not directly answering questions asked or commenting on the points raised. Yes, if you are. It is a good idea to

quote relevant text from the e-mail just to let the recipient know which issues you are addressing.

'Reply All' - gaffe

Inadvertent use of 'Reply All' has caused some major gaffes in the virtual world. Once a woman employee in my office replied to my e-mail asking about attending a party later that week. She hit 'Reply All' while wondering what she should wear; whether to be a good girl and wear sensible clothes or she asked jokingly whether she should shock her colleagues. The responses from other employees almost made her go underground for a few days. Some were in good humour and some outrageous!

To, From, Cc, Bcc, RR

- Only use Cc (Courtesy Copy) when it is important for those you Cc to know about the contents of the e-mail.
- It is not polite to use Return Receipt (RR) on every single e-mail. Doing so is viewed as intrusive, annoying and can be declined by the other side anyway.
- Include addresses in the To: field for those who you would like a response from. Include addresses in the Cc field for those who you are just wishing to add as FYI.
- Make sure your name is displayed properly in the From: field.
- Think about your motives when adding addresses to To:, Cc: and Bcc:. Use your discretion. Remove addresses from the To:, Cc: and Bcc: fields that don't need to see your reply. The Bcc: field is useful where discretion is required. People in this field are concealed from other recipients in the To:, Cc: and Bcc: fields. They can themselves see others in the To: and Cc: fields but not others in the Bcc: fields.

- Be very careful how you use 'Reply All' and Cc: in a business environment. Doing so for the sake of safety or to slyly tattle can backfire and have you viewed as petty or insecure. Make sure when using Bcc: that your intentions are proper. To send Bcc: copies to others, as a way of talking behind someone's back is rude.
- When replying to an e-mail with multiple recipients noted in the To: or Cc: fields, remove the addresses of those who your reply does not apply to.
- Never expose your friend's or contact's e-mail address to strangers by listing them all in the To: field. Instead, use Bcc:!

Forwarding e-mails

- Don't forward e-mails that read like chain letters of yore promising incredible riches or asking your help for a charitable cause. Even if the content seems to be bona fide, the senders are usually not. Since it is impossible to find out whether a chain letter is real or not, the best place for it is the recycle bin.
- If someone asks you not to forward their e-mails, respect that right and desist from forwarding. There is no need to take it personally.
- When forwarding e-mail, take time to type a personal comment to the person you are forwarding to, otherwise don't bother to forward.
- Don't forward anything without editing out all the forwarding >>>>, other e-mail addresses, headers and commentary from all the other forwarders.
- If you must forward to more than one person, put your e-mail address in the To: field and all the others you are

sending to in the Bcc: field to protect their e-mail addresses from being published to those they do not know. This is a serious privacy issue!

- Be careful when forwarding e-mail on political or controversial issues. The recipient may not appreciate your point of view.

Avoid flaming

Flaming e-mail is an e-mail sent as a quick emotional and generally fuming response to an e-mail. It is the often deliberate act of posting or writing messages on Internet bulletin boards and message groups that have the intent of insulting or creating dissent within a group. It can also be sent to some individual.

As you are sitting alone with your computer or mobile, it is easy to go completely berserk when replying to some e-mail that offends you. If you do that and send such a searing e-mail, then you are guilty of flaming.

Flaming has a technical name, the 'online disinhibition effect', which the psychologists apply to the many ways people behave with less restraint in cyberspace.

In a 2004 article in the journal, Cyber Psychology & Behaviour, John Suler, a psychologist at the Rider University in Lawrenceville, N.J., suggested that several psychological factors lead to online disinhibition: the anonymity of a Web pseudonym; invisibility to others; the time lag between sending an e-mail message and getting feedback; the exaggerated sense of self from being alone; and the lack of any online authority figure. Dr. Suler notes that disinhibition can be either benign – when a shy person feels free to open up online – or toxic, as in flaming.

So, think before you click 'Send'.

If you find yourself writing in anger, save a draft, go get a cup of coffee, clear your mind, write the e-mail, delete and write again in a better frame of mind.

Read it again and think if you were in the recipient's place what would you feel? Try to understand the other person. If someone is upset, there is a reason. The faster you discover it and resolve the problem, the faster the situation settles down. Focus on solutions, not your anger.

Before you hit that Reply button and begin keying in an instant emotional response that you may later regret, sit back and carefully reread the e-mail you are responding to making sure to take in its intent in its entirety. Read it out loud – word for word – and you may find that your perception changes. If you react emotionally to one part of an e-mail without looking at the message as a whole, you might perceive the senders meaning out of context.

If you have to give a reply right away, just answer, *"Thank you. Let me get back to you on that."* Don't commit, agree or disagree. Just let the person know you'll look into the situation and write, nothing else. When the time comes for a better reply, never write e-mails with lengthy explanations and justifications. Stick to dealing with the core of the matter and not your own feelings.

Formatting E-mails

- Do not type in ALLCAPS. It is difficult to read and moreover it is perceived as shouting or yelling.
- Do not use patterned backgrounds. Makes your e-mail harder to read.
- Stay away from fancy unusual and uncommon fonts – only the standard fonts are on all computers.

- Use emoticons sparingly to ensure your tone and intent are clear.
- Typing your e-mails in all small case gives the perception of lack of education or laziness.
- Refrain from using multiple font colours in one e-mail. It makes your e-mail harder to view and can add to your intent being misinterpreted.
- Use formatting sparingly. Instead try to rely on choosing the most accurate words possible to reflect your tone and avoid misunderstandings in the process.

E-mails can become embarrassing

Here is a very curious case of a shopper at GASP store in Australia. GASP is a leading fashion house in Australia. The website claims, "As an Australian fashion house, it is important for us to not only source and create pieces that are exceedingly directional, but also remain highly exclusive through our strictly limited production runs." The following news article is from http://www.news.com.au/national/customer-complaint-e-mail-and-response-by-gasp-clothing-goes-viral.

Keara O'Neil was on a shopping trip to find bridesmaid dresses for her wedding and a frock for her hens' night at the GASP Chapel St. store on September 24 when she had a dispute with a sales assistant named 'Chris'.

O'Neil, a retail assistant herself, claims Chris was initially helpful but soon turned nasty, making a dig at her size 12 frame and yelling out as she left the store, *"Have fun shopping at Supre... I knew you were a joke the minute you walked in."*

Distressed by the treatment, O'Neil then sent a letter to the customer service centre at GASP, which was answered by GASP area manager, Matthew Chidgey.

In the e-mail, O'Neil was told the fashion chain aims to appeal *"to a very fashion-forward consumer"* and that the sales assistant, O'Neil made a complaint about a 'retail superstar' who's 'only problem is that he is too good at what he does'.

It went on to say, *"As I am sure you are aware, people who are talented, generally do not tolerate having their time wasted, which is the reason you were provoked to leave the store..."*

"...we respectfully ask that you side step our store."

Mr. Chidgey confirmed today that the e-mail was legitimate.

Later, GASP released a statement defending its response.

"We respect that not all consumers strive for a glamorous appearance; some prefer to simply blend in," the statement said.

"We respect and welcome all the customers, who wish to visit our store, even though the intention to buy may not exist. But we ask that their opinions be expressed through blogs, social media or around a warm latte, but certainly not inside our stores."

It is understood GASP closed its Facebook page following a deluge of negative comments concerning the incident.

***

Take care

Some suggestions for avoiding blunders

- Enter the recipient's e-mail address only when your e-mail is ready to be sent. This helps to reduce the risk of an embarrassing misfire, such as sending an important e-mail to the wrong person or e-mailing a half-written note.

- Attachments may be forgotten. It is a good idea to attach the file before writing the e-mail. This eliminates the embarrassing mistake of forgetting it before hitting 'send', and having to send another e-mail saying you forgot to attach the document. If you double-check an attachment immediately before sending and decide that you need to make changes, don't forget to update the source file. Making corrections to the version that is attached to the e-mail does not often work, and it can lead to different versions of the same document floating around.
- Do not depend too much on e-mails. No one is sitting around staring at their inbox waiting for your e-mail. If something is urgent, use other means of communication. A red 'rush' exclamation point doesn't compare to getting up from your desk or using the phone.
- Generally, people will have one business e-mail address and one for personal e-mails. If you do not have, then get a different one for business.

***

DOH – the Creative Group – conducted a survey on e-mail gaffes. Here are some responses:

- *"Someone sent out confidential salary information to the whole firm."*
- *"I once sent a job offer to the wrong person."*
- *"An employee sent his resumé to me by mistake. It was supposed to go to an outside company."*
- *"Someone made a nasty comment about a supervisor and it was sent to the supervisor by mistake. It eventually led to dismissal."*

- *"A person called another employee an idiot in an e-mail to everyone in the company."*
- *"One of our vendors accidentally e-mailed me information about their sales performance, so I gained some inside knowledge about that vendor."*
- *"My receptionist sent a very gossipy and catty e-mail about another employee to the wrong person. It was so unprofessional that she was terminated."*
- *"We sent an e-mail to a client that was meant for a vendor. It made things all the more difficult when the client had seen our costs."*
- *"Confidential information about one client was sent to a different client. It was certainly embarrassing."*
- *"Someone crafted a scathing, sarcastic e-mail about a customer and did not mean to hit 'Send.' It caused problems."*
- *"I once sent an internal memo about restroom etiquette to a prospective client by accident."*
- *"Someone sent me a copy of an employee's bank records by mistake."*
- *"Someone meant to send a racy picture to a couple of friends but ended up sending it to the entire staff, which caused her much embarrassment."*

They advise giving your e-mail undivided attention. Avoid multitasking when responding to important or sensitive messages. If you can't respond right away, let the person know when they can expect to hear back. Then, compose the e-mail when you're free of distractions. Reread and only when you are sure, hit 'Send'!

❐

Listening

Communication is complete only when one speaks and others listen. Listening is, in fact, a very important aspect of communication and often neglected. The argument is *"What's so great about learning to listen? We all listen, don't we?"* No! *We all hear* is more accurate. Listening involves more than just hearing.

How often have you wondered if the person you are talking to is indeed listening? And how often have you listened to people talking to you? There have been many research studies on this subject. Depending on the study being quoted, you remember between 25% and 50% of what you hear. That means that when you talk to your boss, colleagues, customers or family members for ten minutes, they pay attention to less than half of the conversation. Also when you are receiving directions or being presented with information, you aren't hearing the whole message either. You hope the important parts are captured in your 25-50%, but what if they are not?

I have this problem with my husband. He just doesn't listen. Many times I land up saying in exasperation, *"You haven't been listening to me!"* Once I said something outrageous and commented that he has not been listening.

"I have been!" He protested.

"Okay, so give me the money."

Instead of asking for what, smart that he is, he said, *"How much?"*

"About a lakh and a half would do!"

He gasped, *"What?!"*

I patiently explained, (now I had his full attention), *"For the diamond studs that you said I could buy!"*

"I did?"

"Yes, when I asked, you said 'uh…oh'. Isn't that yes?"

After this incident (I did not get money to buy diamond studs!), he began to listen, not just hear. Of course, that reverted to normal pretty soon. However, such routine 'hearing but not listening' would not be an advantage at work or with friends! Work would suffer, colleagues would snigger and friends would prefer to stay away!

Many times, this kind of mechanical hearing gives rise to misunderstandings and conflicts. Therefore, it becomes essential to cultivate good listening habit! By becoming a better listener, you will improve your productivity, as well as your ability to influence, persuade and negotiate. All of these are necessary for workplace as well as social success!

Some are natural listeners; counsellors refine their listening skills and the rest of us need to learn to listen. If we listen with the correct attitude and right approach, then we can listen our way to success. Good listening is an art. It needs the presence of mind, passion, patience and practice. In fact, a person can speak @ 100 to 200 words per minute, but the brain can process words much faster. It is up to us to utilise this time to concentrate on the speaker and review the message or to let the mind wander.

French, writer Francois (the second duc de) la Rochefoucauld's take on conversation is interesting. He says, "*One reason why we find so few people who are rational and agreeable in conversation is that there is hardly anyone who does not think more about what he wants to say than about responding to what is said. The most clever and polite people are content with merely seeming attentive – and we can perceive in their eyes and mind that they are wandering from what is said, and want to return to what they want to say; instead of considering that the worst way to persuade or please others is to try to please ourselves [this way], and that listening well and answering well are some of the greatest charms we can have in conversation.*"

So, how to achieve this? You have already taken the first step. You have become conscious of 'listening'. It is more than mechanical hearing. I read a great definition of listening … it is hearing with intention. The way to become a better listener is to make a conscious effort to hear not only the words that another person is saying but, more importantly, try to understand the complete message being conveyed. In order to do this, you must pay attention to the other person very carefully, and not let your attention wander nor begin forming counter-arguments in your mind and wait to rebut!

What does it mean to really listen?

Real listening is an active process that has five basic activities.

1. Sensing: Physically hearing the message and taking note of it. Hearing just means listening to the sound of the speaker talking. Like listening to music while reading a book, it is more awareness than understanding.

2. Interpreting: Decoding and absorbing what one hears. The listener concentrates on what is being said. It happens when you take in what you have heard and understand it in your own way. The speaker's frame of reference may be quite different. What exactly does she mean? This is where understanding begins.
3. Evaluating: Forming an opinion about the message. After you are sure you understand what the speaker has said, think about whether it makes sense. Sorting out the exact message can become difficult. Also dismissing what an unimpressive speaker says and agreeing with an attractive and forceful speaker is easy.
4. Remembering: Saving a message for future reference. Actual or mental notes will help in retaining the information.
5. Responding: Acknowledging the message by reacting in some way.

***

Listening can make our loved ones feel worthy, appreciated, interesting and respected. When we listen, we encourage others to listen to us. Ordinary conversations emerge on a deeper level, as do our relationships.

In our love relationships, greater communication brings greater intimacy. Parents' listening to their kids helps build the latter's self-esteem. In the business world, listening saves time and money by preventing misunderstandings. And we always learn more when we listen than when we talk. Listening skills ensure our social, emotional and professional success, and studies prove that listening is a skill we can learn.

To enhance your listening skills, you need to let the other person know that you are listening to what he or she is saying. Acknowledgement can be something as simple as a nod of the head or a simple 'uh huh'. That does not mean your acquiescence with the speaker, but just an indication that you are listening and absorbing. Using body language and other signs to acknowledge you are listening also reminds you to pay attention and not let your mind wander.

It takes a lot of concentration and determination to be an active listener. Be deliberate with your listening and keep in mind that you really want to hear what the other person is saying. Set aside all other thoughts to focus on the message. Ask questions, reflect, and paraphrase to ensure you understand the message. If you don't, then you'll find that what someone says to you and what you hear can be amazingly different!

How to listen actively?

Active listening is really an extension of the Golden Rule. To know how to listen to someone else, think about how you would want to be listened to.

While the ideas are largely intuitive, it might take some practice to develop or brush up listening skills. Here are some suggestions:

1. Face the speaker. Sit up straight or lean forward slightly to show your attentiveness through body language.
2. Maintain eye contact to the degree that you all remain relaxed. This does not mean staring hard so as to make the speaker uncomfortable.
3. Minimize external distractions. Turn off the TV. Put down your book or magazine, and ask the speaker and other listeners to do the same.

4. Respond appropriately to show that you understand. Murmur ('uh-huh' and 'um-hmm') and nod. Raise your eyebrows. Say words such as *"Really"*,*"Interesting"*, as well as more direct prompts: *"What did you do then?"* and *"What did she say?"*

5. Focus solely on what the speaker is saying. Try not to think about what you are going to say next. The conversation will follow a logical flow after the speaker makes her point.

6. Minimize internal distractions. If your own thoughts keep distracting you, simply let them go and continuously re-focus your attention on the speaker, much as you would during meditation.

7. Keep an open mind. Wait until the speaker is finished before deciding that you disagree. Try not to make assumptions about what the speaker is thinking.

8. Avoid letting the speaker know how you handled a similar situation. Unless they specifically ask for advice; assume that they just need to talk it out.

9. Even if the speaker is launching a complaint against you, wait until he finishes before defending yourself. The speaker will feel as though his point had been made. He won't feel the need to repeat it, and you'll know the whole argument before you respond. Research shows that, on an average, we can hear four times faster than we can talk, so we have the ability to sort ideas as they come in and be ready for more.

10. Engage yourself. Ask questions for clarification, but, once again, wait until the speaker has finished. That

way, you won't interrupt their train of thought. After you ask questions, paraphrase their point to make sure you didn't misunderstand. Start with: "So, *you're saying...*"

As you work on developing your listening skills, you may feel a bit panicky when there is a natural pause in the conversation. What should you say next? Learn to settle into the silence and use it to better understand all points of view better.

As your listening skills improve, so will your aptitude for conversation. I get complimented often on my conversational skills. However, I do not talk much, but listen actively. Maybe that is because I am genuinely interested in what the other person is saying.

Reasons for not listening

1. Prejudice against the speaker: Sometimes, the attitude of the speakers or their personality conflicts with our attitude. At such times, it is difficult to concentrate on what they are saying.
2. External distractions: Does the speaker talk too strident? Make excessive gestures? Wear loud clothes? Dress sloppy? Any of this can tune you out. Actually, the entire physical environment can prove disturbing.
3. Thinking speed: Research shows that the speaking speed of even fast speakers is phenomenally less than that of thinking speed. So, a listener will always have time on his hand. What do you do then? Let your mind wander? Shift your attention elsewhere? Daydream? You could easily miss out on important points in the speaker's message.

4. Hasty assessment: How often have you interrupted others? Finished their sentences? Prompted their conclusions? As all of us think fast, we race ahead to what we feel is the conclusion. The conclusion we arrive at could be different from what the speaker intended.
5. Semantic Stereotypes: Some words irritate us, as do some people without any obvious reason. Which words do you like and why? Which words bother you and why? We carry our prejudices and feelings within us. We tune out the speaker due to some words or even gestures we don't like.
6. Delivery: A monotone can put the listeners to sleep. The delivery of the speech can be annoying, making the listeners bored, distracted, and critical of the message. 'So boring' is generally a critique of the delivery than an assessment of a speaker's mental abilities.

***

Barriers to Listening

Some barriers are attributed to the speaker, some to the environment and rest to the listener. While the listeners can do little to combat the first two, they can and should try to smoothen out the third type.

Speaker barriers:

- Speaker mumbles, is not coherent, is monotonous
- Speaker uses confusing technical jargon or inflammatory words
- Speaker is ambiguous, uses words with different interpretation

- Speaker's attitude, knowledge, information and motives may not be appealing to the listener
- Speaker's inability to say helpful things
- Speaker's state of mind
- Speaker's speed of talking may be too fast

Environment barriers

- Distracting noise
- Interruptions

Listener barriers

- Listener is tired or uncomfortable
- Doesn't like the speaker's manner, appearance, tone of voice, etc.
- Is tempted to skip the difficult
- Listener is trying to take down extensive notes and misses points
- Uninterested and has preconceived ideas
- Thinks he knows more than the speaker
- Is afraid, envious or prejudiced about the speaker
- Wants to give his own ideas
- Listener's over-sensitiveness to some words or phrases
- Listener's ideas are in contradiction to the speakers and, hence, cannot accept
- Listener's deaf spots prevent him from listening to some phrases and subjects
- Concentration, understanding and objective evaluation is lacking

- Some listeners are constantly trying to find counter-arguments to everything the speaker is saying

***

Listening is difficult, as it does not occur in isolation. There is a continuous stream of consciousness in the listener's head made up partly of understanding and interpretation of what he is hearing, partly of associations and connections, and partly of other preoccupations and interests that may have nothing to do with the external dialogue. Also there is a risk that what the speaker is saying has to compete for attention with what is going on independently in the listener's mind. Clearing your mind is crucial.

So, be a good listener to be a good communicator.....!!

❒

Appendix

COMMUNICATION BASICS

Communication is the most important process of Nature, more so for humans! We require communication in our personal lives, in our social lives and also in our careers. It helps not only to fulfil our needs but also makes every relationship and every task smooth. All these communication processes are based on the premise that communication is exchange of information. The objective of Communication is:

- To be received (Heard or read).
- To be understood.
- To be accepted.
- To get action (Change behaviour or attitude).

Communication is a continuous and complex process that requires constant attention. In whichever form, communication has to be lucid, conveying the exact meaning with no scope for misunderstanding.

Let us have a look at the process of 'Interpersonal communication'. This is because all the communication including corporate communication finally stems from this process. To understand this process, let us first know the basics.

Communication means transmitting and receiving verbal/ non-verbal messages.

Process of communication

Sender >> Message >> Medium >> Receiver >> Feedback

Sender

When you send a message, you are the encoder. You choose words/symbols that will correctly and tactfully express your message to the receiver without any ambiguity, and elicit desired reaction.

An external stimulus prompts you to send a message: a business transaction, query, meetings, interviews, favours....

Your ideas are influenced by:

- Your external environment: physical surroundings, weather, noise, discomforts, and cultural customs.
- Your internal stimuli: attitudes, likes/dislikes, opinions, emotions, experiences, education, job status, and your perception of the receiver's needs, skills, understanding, experience.

Message

Verbal/non-verbal messages should give due consideration to content, how the receiver will interpret it and how it will affect the future course of action.

Media

In addition to the traditional oral and written communication, the field now increasingly encompasses telephones, faxes, e-mails, and other technological advances, such as cellphones and laptops! It has become simpler and faster to communicate virtually with anybody, anywhere as long as common media exist.

Receiver

The receiver is also the decoder of the message. Here too the perception of the receiver is influenced by external and internal stimuli as in the case of the encoder. Each receiver through his/her receptor mechanisms perceives the intended meaning of the sender's idea.

Feedback

The response of the receiver is based on his/her interpretation of the message. It could be oral, written or action-based. The success or failure of the communication is indicated by the response activated.

***

Rather than connecting via just one form of communication, professionals are creating 'media-kits' that enable them to select exactly the right medium for a particular task. As communication options and needs increase, clear preferences have emerged regarding the best ways to exchange specific types of information. The modern communications tool belt includes:

- Phone and Audio Conferences: Conveying complex information clearly, clarifying meaning, collaborating, building relationships, priority communications
- Video and Web Conferences: Brainstorming, collaboration, planning, presentations
- E-mail: Check-ins, status reports, follow-up, group communications, attachments
- IM: Presence information, check-in (*"Are you there?"*), simple query

- Text (SMS): Uncomplicated time-sensitive information
- Social Media: Networking, news updates

Check for Completeness

- Remember the five Ws - what, why, when, where, who; and also how
- Have you given all the facts?
- Have you covered the essentials?
- Have you answered all the questions - straight and implied?
- Have you given something extra?

Check for Correctness

- Are all the facts correct?
- Have you confirmed the reader's name?
- Are all numbers absolutely correct?
- Is the message grammatically correct?

Check for Conciseness

- Have you plunged right into the subject of the message?
- Have you avoided rehashing the reader's letter?
- Have you used one word instead of a phrase, one sentence instead of two?
- Have you said enough, but just enough?
- Have you avoided needless 'filler' words and phrases?
- Is all the material really relevant?
- Are buzzwords, trite expressions absent?

Check for Consideration

- Have you looked at things from the reader's point of view?
- Does your message show reader benefit and emphasise what they want to know?
- Have you protected the reader's ego?
- Is your focus on the positive side?
- Have you remembered that your audience is human?
- Have you maintained proper etiquette?
- Is the message evidently critical? Rewrite!

Check for Concreteness

- Were you precise in using facts and figures whenever possible?
- Did you use active voice more than passive?
- Is there action in verbs rather than in nouns?
- Did you try to use vivid, image-building words occasionally?

But in business writing, use them sparingly.

Check for Clarity

- Are the words precise and concrete?
- Are the words appropriate for the intended audience?
- Have you used familiar words?
- Is the sentence lesser than 15 words?
- Are the words arranged to give a clear idea of the main topic?

Check for Courtesy

- Does your message have a sincere 'you attitude'?
- Is it tactful and thoughtful?
- Is the tone right for the subject?
- Does it use positive and respectful words?
- Is the language non-discriminatory?

JARGON AND BUZZWORDS

Jargon is the specialised language of a particular field, trade, social or cultural group, occupation, or profession - information technology, the military, government, Psychology, Economics, Mathematics, Biology, Medicine, and so on. When you are writing a paper in a particular field, you can use these specialised terms that are accepted and understood in that field. Or if your recipient also belongs to the same field, jargon can be used.

Buzzwords are terms that have spread beyond their original field, and people outside the occupation often use the words imprecisely or pretentiously, for example: downsize, cutting edge, holistic, benchmarking, paradigm, synergy, tipping point, off-shoring, next generation.

Buzzwords such as 'basically' may indicate that you are talking down to the receiver. It implies, *"I know more than what I am saying. I have made it simpler for you to help you understand."*

Buzzwords over-generalise a subject in an attempt to make the speaker's content appear more significant than it is. They are a fake display of greatness, and they are often born of the same kind of fears.

CONTEXTUAL MEANINGS

Conceptual meaning (logical, cognitive, or denotative content), connotative meaning (what is communicated by virtue of what language refers to), social meaning (what is communicated of the social circumstances of language use), effective meaning (what is communicated of the feeling and attitudes of the speaker/writer), reflected meaning (what is communicated through association with another sense of the same expression), collocative meaning (what is communicated through association with words which tend to occur in the environment of another world), thematic meaning (what is communicated by the way in which the message is organized in terms of order and emphasis).

WORK COMMUNICATION

Work communication needs to initiate with face-to-face communication. This is especially so for the last step in the chain of command. The employees who would be performing the actual tasks need to be informed in person. All the pros and cons, the deliverables, the required equipment and support, team composition, each member's task and other necessary points have to be discussed face-to-face. This discussion, of course, has to be supported by a work document.

For the sake of simplicity and comprehension, a work instruction sheet should contain the following elements:

- From:
- To:
- Project:
- Deliverables:

- Completion date:
- Schedule of meetings:
- Team composition:
- Skill-sets required for the task in hand:
- Training required:
- Your share of work in the entire project:
- Equipment, support needed and available:
- Completion date for your contribution:
- Week-wise work schedule:
- Date-wise work schedule:
- Today's schedule:

Once a detailed map of the project is made available to each worker, then his/her task becomes simpler.

So, in addition to ensuring the seven Cs of effective communication, maintaining simple work map will ensure timely completion of every new project.

CHANGE COMMUNICATION AT ITS MOST BASIC

Why change?

The rationale behind the change and what is involved.

Who will inform?

CEO or MD in an open meeting or direct supervisor in person.

How to communicate?

Face-to-face is the best way.

What to communicate?

- What is involved and what is the expected action?
- What is in it for the employee?

When to communicate?

- Before the change, during and frequently about change.
- Work-related whenever required.

Guidelines/Suggestions for maintaining a communication document during change

Table 1: Communication Document

What	Who	To Whom	When	**Where**	**How**
Major Change Announcement	CEO/MD	All	Before Imple-mentation	Open Forum	Face-to-face Meeting
Reviews and News	CEO/MD	All	Quarterly	Open Forum E-mails	Face-to-face Meeting E-mails
Project Work	Project Leader	Team Mates	When Required	Cabin/ Conference Room E-mails	Face-to-face Meeting E-mails
Action Items/ Statement of Work	Team Leader	Team Mates	Start of Project	Cabin/ Conference Room E-mail	Face-to-face Meeting E-mails
Interim Status Report	Team Members	Team Leader	Planned Intervals	E-mails/ Phone Calls	E-mails/ Phone Calls
Status Report	Team Leader	Project Leader/ Client	Planned Intervals	Video/ Audio Conference or E-mails	Conference Room/E-mails
Project Deliverables	Team Leader	Project Leader/ Client	End of Project	Client Facility/ E-mail	As Decided

Frank Visco usually receives credit (when given at all) as the primary author of the list. Some have claimed it is actually lifted from William Safire, who is understood to have written similar material. It may have evolved from a variety of sources. William Safire's list is given next.

HOW TO WRITE GOOD

Frank L. Visco

My several years in the word game have taught me several rules:

- Avoid alliteration. Always!
- Prepositions are not words to end sentences with.
- Avoid clichés like the plague. (They are old hat!)
- Employ the vernacular.
- Eschew ampersands and abbreviations, etc.
- Parenthetical remarks (however relevant) are unnecessary.
- It is wrong to ever split an infinitive.
- Contractions are not necessary.
- Foreign words and phrases are not apropos.
- One should never generalize.
- Eliminate quotations. As Ralph Waldo Emerson once said: *"I hate quotations. Tell me what you know."*
- Comparisons are as bad as clichés.
- Don't be redundant; don't use words more than necessary; it is highly superfluous.
- Profanity sucks.

- Be more or less specific.
- Understatement is always the best.
- Exaggeration is a billion times worse than understatement.
- One-word sentences?! Eliminate.
- Analogies in writing are like feathers on a snake.
- The passive voice is to be avoided.
- Go around the barn at high noon to avoid colloquialisms.
- Even if a mixed metaphor sings, it should be derailed.
- Who needs rhetorical questions?

SOME POINTERS FOR GOOD WRITING BY WILLIAM SAFIRE

- Parenthetical words, however, must be enclosed in commas.
- It behooves you to avoid archaic expressions.
- Avoid archaeic spellings too.
- Don't repeat yourself, or say again what you have said before.
- Don't use commas, that, are not, necessary.
- Do not use hyperbole; not one in a million can do it effectively.
- Never use a big word when a diminutive alternative would suffice.
- Subject and verb always has to agree.
- Placing a comma between subject and predicate, is not correct.

- Use youre spell chekker to avoid mispeling and to catch typograhpical errers.
- Use the apostrophe in it's proper place and omit it when its not needed.
- Don't never use no double negatives.
- Poofread carefully to see if you any words out.
- Hopefully, you will use words correctly, irregardless of how others use them.
- Eschew obfuscation.
- No sentence fragments.
- Don't indulge in sesquipedalian lexicological constructions.
- A writer must not shift your point of view.
- Don't overuse exclamation marks!!
- Place pronouns as close as possible, especially in long sentences, as of 10 or more words, to their antecedents.
- Writing carefully, dangling participles must be avoided.
- If any word is improper at the end of a sentence, a linking verb is.
- Avoid trendy locutions that sound flaky.
- Everyone should be careful to use a singular pronoun with singular nouns in their writing.
- Always pick on the correct idiom.
- The adverb always follows the verb.
- Take the bull by the hand and avoid mixing metaphors.
- If you reread your work, you can find on re-reading a great deal of repetition can be by rereading and editing.
- And always be sure to finish what

SOME NETIQUETTES

- Read the e-mail before you send it. A lot of people don't bother to read an e-mail before they send it out, as can be seen from the many spelling and grammar mistakes contained in e-mails. Apart from this, reading your e-mail through the eyes of the recipient will help you send a more effective message and avoid misunderstandings and inappropriate comments. Pre-set spell-check on your e-mail application. It gives you the option to correct spelling as you write or send it anyway.
- Take care of abbreviations and emoticons. In business e-mails, try not to use abbreviations such as BTW (by the way) and LOL (laughing out loud). The recipient might not be aware of the meanings of the abbreviations and in business e-mails, these are generally not appropriate. The same goes for emoticons, such as the smiley :-). If you are not sure whether your recipient knows what it means, it is better not to use it.
- Do not use e-mail to convey confidential information.
- Sending an e-mail is like sending an open letter. Never make any libellous, sexist or racially discriminating comments in e-mails, even if they are meant to be a joke.
- Try not to make assumptions when it comes to e-mail. Always ask for clarification before you react.
- Even if you mark 'confidential', e-mails are forwarded to others. Keep this in mind when typing about emotional or controversial topics.
- When there is a misunderstanding created by an e-mail, don't hesitate to pick up the old-fashioned telephone to work things out! Also send a follow-up e-mail confirming the conversation.

- Know that how you type, and the efforts you make or don't make will indicate what is important to you and if you are an educated courteous person.
- If a friend puts your e-mail address in the To: field with others you do not know, ask them to no longer expose your address to strangers without your permission.
- Call first and then write confirmation e-mail.

BUSINESS E-MAIL

- Think of your business e-mail as though it was on your business letterhead and you will not go wrong.
- If you cannot respond to an e-mail promptly, e-mail back confirming your receipt and convey when the sender can expect your response.
- E-mailing site owners about your product or service through the site form is still spam. Ask them if they want more information first.
- When replying to e-mails, always respond promptly and edit out unnecessary information from the post you are responding.
- Formality is in place as a courtesy and reflects respect. Assume the highest level of formality with new e-mail contacts until the relationship dictates otherwise. Refrain from getting too informal too soon in your e-mail communications.
- Never send anyone an e-mail they need to unsubscribe from when they didn't subscribe in the first place!
- Never send business attachments outside of business hours and confirm that the other side can open the format in which you send.

- Before getting upset because you perceive someone didn't respond, check to see if their reply was inadvertently deleted or sent to your Trash or Junk folder.
- Feel free to modify the Subject: field to more accurately reflect a conversation's direction. Sometimes, if you keep the same subject while hitting 'Reply' and embark on an entirely new issue, the recipient will be confused.
- When it comes to your e-mail communications, know who you can trust and trust only those you know.
- Take the time to review each e-mail before clicking 'Send' to ensure that your message is clear and you are relaying the tone that you desire.
- Always add the e-mail addresses of Websites and new contacts immediately to your approved senders or address book so they get through the Spam filters.
- Before completing a Website's Contact form, make an effort to review the site to be sure the information you seek is not already available.
- Take a quick look at the e-mails in your Trash before you delete them just in case a good e-mail landed there by mistake.
- Don't mass e-mail people who didn't ask to be on your personal 'mailing list'.

❑❑❑